Blacksmithing Made Easy for Beginners

A Step-by-Step Introduction to Blacksmithing for Beginners to Help you Perfect the Art of Blacksmithing

Introduction

Blacksmithing is a combined craft and an art as well. When the industrial revolution began in the 1800s, many predicted the craft would face extinction. The metal and steel products blacksmiths crafted previously began being mass-produced by the emerging industries at the time, and it seemingly sounded the death knell for the industry.

Fortunately, the predictions of doom did not come to pass, and blacksmithing has stood the test of time. Surprisingly, blacksmithing skills have witnessed a rebirth and increased demand today.

Whether you want to take up blacksmithing as a hobby, side-hustle, or as your main trade, learning the craft comes with many benefits.

Apart from the rewarding financial aspect, blacksmithing can link you up with numerous other industries such as fishing, hunting, fishing, carpentry, mining, and farming, among several others. Additionally, it can be a stepping stone to the art world of metallic ceramics and sculptures – the possibilities are endless.

This book seeks to support your dream and ambition by being the first step in your thousand-mile journey by providing a solid foundation in blacksmithing. From the basics, where and how to begin, tools, what it takes, to practical beginner projects, described in simple, factual, enjoyable, and comprehensively. Also, your level of experience with iron, steel, and related tools of this ancient noble craft matters little because this book will exhaustively cover all the important lessons.

By the end of this book, you should have the know-how to set up a blacksmithing workshop and have all the information you need to mold metal into a unique piece of art.

PS: I'd like your feedback. If you are happy with this book, please leave a review on Amazon.

Please leave a review for this book on Amazon by visiting the page below:

https://amzn.to/2VMR5qr

Table of Contents

Chapter 1: Blacksmithing in a Nutshell

Once you learn blacksmithing, the craft, you will be referred to as a 'blacksmith.' This is a combination of two words, 'black' and 'smith.' Black originates from the color metal turns into after it is heated or forged. A black layer of oxide forms on the metal's surface during the forging process. On the other hand, 'Smith' refers to 'smite' or hit.

Therefore, a blacksmith is a person who hits black metal, literally.

What Does Blacksmithing Entail?

Generally, a blacksmith's job is to forge steel to create various metallic objects. Forging is *'making or shaping a metallic object by heating it in a fire or furnace and hammering it.'* This is a word you will encounter numerous times as you learn the basic tenets of blacksmithing, and it is important to understand its meaning from the onset. Also, the craft essentially revolves around the forging of metal.

If you have the passion and a creative eye to shape plain metal into beautiful everyday objects, these are all the qualifications you need to begin the blacksmithing learning process.

Many blacksmiths opt to remain self-employed, owing to the flexibility and creative freedom this arrangement offers. When you eventually begin your blacksmithing business, you can start small, probably honing your skills from home and growing from there.

Apart from making common products such as household items, tools, gates, railings, rims, nails, candlesticks, and others, there is also a lot of demand for niche products such as knives, swords, armors, shields, to mention a few.

Blacksmithing opportunities are not only restricted to self-employment; formal employment in mid and large-sized metal and steel companies is also available. If you choose to go this route, you will have the chance to work on large projects and become part of a team. Additionally, you will gain experience, learn fast, attain financial stability, and witness first-hand how industry professionals run the business.

Some of the job opportunities available in industries directly related to blacksmithing include;

- Forging machine operators

- Bending machine operator

- Upsetter operator

- Cold drawn operator

- Trip hammer operator

- Cold press operator

- Manipulator operator

- Forging press operator

- Hot press operator

To become an accomplished blacksmith, you will develop some essential skills along the way, like problem-solving and many other skills. These skills will help you maneuver easily and quickly as you work, and with time, they will be like second nature, always kicking in automatically. Some of the skills include;

- The ability to spot potential problems in the course of blacksmithing and solve them immediately as you work (Fast thinking and problem-solving skills)

- Ability to observe the color of a piece of metal and decide the best time to begin forging it (making decisions)

- Refer to manuals and other reading materials when in doubt about certain operations of equipment and proper setup (research skills)

- Making and completing measurements accurately (Numerical skills)

- Thinking in a step-based format when planning projects (Job organizing and task planning)

The positive part is that these skills are transferable and usable under different circumstances away from blacksmithing —they are also teachable to others. Additionally, the newly acquired skill-sets last a lifetime.

Ways to Become a Blacksmith

For every destination, there are always various roads at your disposal that can lead you there; blacksmithing is no different. Although a few formal educational programs in blacksmithing exist, most blacksmiths are self-trained. It is also worth noting that formal qualifications are not a requirement in this field; skill is all that matters.

College Education

As mentioned earlier, a few institutions offer blacksmithing courses from certificate level to bachelor degrees that last around two years. However, it is time-consuming as most courses are available full-time. The tuition fees are expensive as well.

Additionally, since the institutions that offer the course are few and far between, enrolling and learning in a college may involve long-distance travel; or moving altogether. This can be disruptive, especially if you have to keep a certain job to fund your college education.

Apprenticeship

An apprenticeship is another viable option to learn blacksmithing. It provides practical and hands-on experience. Chances are, you will learn fast and gain experience quickly since all the lessons are practical. Apprenticeships work better when you learn the basics independently.

The downside to this approach is that you have to keep to your 'teacher's' schedule, and learning will not always be consistent. Or you may learn one thing for a long duration, depending on your instructor's job orders.

Self-taught

This is usually the best approach to take because it offers;

- **Flexibility** – You can learn at your own time and pace. In case you do not understand something well, you can always refer back, take another look, and see what you missed

- **Inexpensive** - Apart from the cost of the learning material, in this case, a book, you save on tuition, transport, and valuable time

- **Practicality** – It is possible to learn from the confines of your home, and the practical lessons are in a stress-free environment that you are comfortable and well-conversant with; and under no pressure

- **Progress** – A self-taught student dictates the pace of progress which depends on individual learning speed capacity. In classroom settings, students learn collectively without considering individual capabilities and limitations. Here, control of the learning progress is solely in your hands

Common Terms Used in Blacksmithing

Throughout this book, you will encounter some terminologies commonly used in blacksmithing. It's best to learn about them, what they refer to, and their context usage to make the learning process simple but also comprehensive.

Hammering and Forging

You are already aware of what forging means, but as a reminder, it is the process of shaping metal by heating it over high temperatures to make it moldable into the end product you desire. Once the piece of metal you are working on is sufficiently heated, the hammering action shapes it.

These two processes form the foundation of the blacksmithing craft. Although we will come to it later, it is worth mentioning right now that the forging temperature and hammering technique largely depend on the specific type of metal you are working on.

For example, the forging temperature of steel is normally between 2150 to 2375 degrees Fahrenheit, while alloy steel ranges from 825-875 degrees Centigrade.

Drawing Out

When working with a piece of metal, you may need to make it thinner, longer, or both. This process is called *drawing out* in blacksmithing. Once you have your piece of metal forged to the required temperature, you can remove it from the 'fire' held by tongs. A tong is a tool used to handle hot metal, which we will look at shortly.

The piece of metal is then placed on an anvil, which is the equivalent of a working bench, and hammered on each side to mold it to the length and thinness required.

Upsetting

If you require a piece of metal you are working on to be narrower, thicker, and shorter, upsetting is the technical term used. Here, just like in drawing out, the piece of metal is heated to its forging temperature, retrieved, placed on the anvil, and hammered until it achieves the desired dimensions.

Experienced blacksmiths often use upsetting because it is technical and requires skill. Some old hands prefer to heat only the specific part of the metal meant for shaping instead of the entire piece.

Punching

Creating holes in a forged piece of metal is called punching, and a punching tool is used.

After forging your hot piece of metal, retrieve it and place it on an anvil. Take the punching tool and bore holes into your piece of metal at a pre-determined spot. Punching is usually done gently to avoid damaging the anvil's surface.

Bending

It is possible to curve a piece of forged metal, which is known as bending. Again, you heat the metal until it reaches its forging temperature. Then, you retrieve it, place it on the anvil, and hammer the parts of the piece of metal where you need to create a bend.

Alternatively, you can forge only sections of the piece of metal that require bends instead of heating the whole piece of metal. The bending process can also be reversed by re-heating the curved piece of metal, hammering it to straighten a bend.

Peening

It is important to protect a metal's surface from corrosion and degradation through *peening*, a process that also guarantees the final product's durability. Peening involves using mechanical force through hammering, which causes tensile and compression stresses. This makes a piece of metal resistant to corrosion, cracks, and other external stresses.

Unlike all the above processes undertaken after forging, peening is done on a cold piece of metal.

As you read this book, you will encounter these terms and processes often as we delve deeper into the world of blacksmithing.

Chapter 2: The Anvil and Measurement Tools

The tools, equipment, and gear used in blacksmithing expedite tasks and simplify the various processes.

Blacksmithing demands a lot of physical exertion, and the right tools are of the utmost importance to enable the successful completion of jobs. Let us look at the tools, equipment, and gear vital to a blacksmith.

Anvil

The anvil is the most conspicuous tool in a blacksmith's workshop. It is a huge metal block with a top, flat surface. This flat top part is where pieces of metal are placed and hammered to mold them into the desired shape.

Anvils are available in numerous shapes and sizes and constructed using a cast or forged steel, translating into highly reinforced steel. This is because the material can withstand years of strikes from a blacksmith's hammer and the high temperatures of forged metal frequently placed on the anvil.

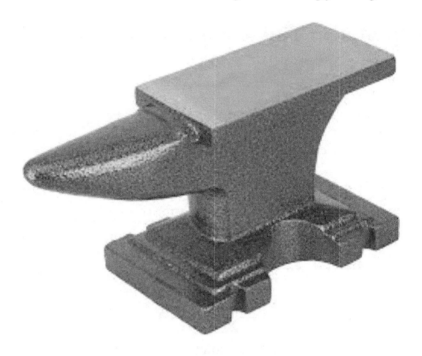

A solid anvil made from cast iron

Quality anvils can weigh up to 440 pounds (200kgs). Also, there is a variety of low-quality and inexpensive anvils made from low-quality steel and carbon. Usually, this variety is not recommended if you intend to engage in serious blacksmithing as the anvils lack rebound when struck and get deformed in record time.

Anvil Positioning

To ensure your anvil's stability while working, it is best to mount it on a pedestal or any other sturdy base. This avoids a situation where you have to reach across to access it – instead, you should always be able to walk around your anvil.

You can use a strong stand made of wood as it will absorb blows, minimize the rebound effect and prevent the anvil from ringing or vibrating. However, metal stands work equally well.

An anvil mounted on a tree stump. An anvil stand ensures stability while working.

Your anvil should be adjusted and positioned based on your height. It becomes difficult to use it if it is either too high or too low, which can strain your muscles. A suitable height protects your back from strain or injury and increases efficiency whenever you swing your hammer.

To achieve the right height for your anvil, use this technique that is popular with masseuses when setting their massage tables;

- Face the anvil while your arms are hanging on both sides

- Clench your fist

- Set the anvil with the height of your knuckles until they are in line with the top flat part of the anvil, also called the face

Anvil Parts

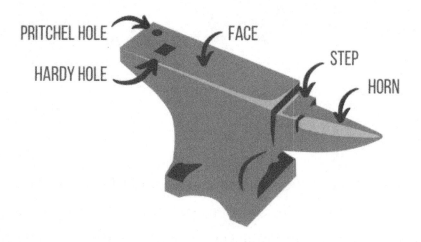

The nomenclature of an anvil.

- **Face** – This is the top part of your anvil mentioned earlier, with a flat and smooth surface. Any piece of metal you are working on is normally placed across the anvil's face —when it is hot enough to be shaped by hammering.

- **Beak/Horn** – This part sticks out at one end of the anvil. Some anvils have a pyramid shape beak/horn on the opposite end. Most of the time, the horn/beak is cone-shaped and used to stretch, round, fold or bend pieces of metal.

- **Hardy hole** – This is a square hole found on the anvil's face. This is referred to as the *hardy hole,* and it is used to hold tools that can cut or form metal pieces. The most common tool that fits into the hole is a hardy, a tool used for cutting metal —it resembles a chisel.

- **Pritchel hole** – A circular hole also located on the anvil's face. The *pritchel hole* is used by blacksmiths when punching holes in metal, for example, when creating a nail hole on a horseshoe. A tool with a spike, called a pritchel, is used for the task. A piece of metal that requires holes to be punched is placed on the hole, and the pritchel is used to bore a hole in the metal. The pritchel hole prevents the spike-like feature of the boring tool from breaking when it comes into contact with the anvil's flat, hard surface.

Although the hardy and pritchel tools are the main tools used in the respective holes, other tools that come in different shapes and sizes can also be used; to mold, cut, punch, bend, twist, and fold metal.

Anvil Usage Tips

- Asses the size, position, and condition of your anvil

- Ensure the anvil's top is clean and clear of any debris before placing a forged piece of metal. Any material leftovers on the anvil's surface can damage the job at hand

- Any tool in the hardy hole that is not in use should be removed. A tool sticking out from the hole is a danger to you; when hammering, you may accidentally hit it with your hand and get injured

Anvil Tools

The Cut-off Hardy

The cut-off hardy is the most common tool used with an anvil, and it is for cutting metal pieces into the required size pieces. The hardy hole on the anvil's face is designed for this tool.

An example of an asymmetrical hardy fixed on the hardy hole of an anvil

How to Use the Cut-off Hardy

- Choose the right size hardy for your anvil

- Carefully fit the tool into the hardy hole located on the anvil's surface, with the edge for cutting facing upwards

- Heat your piece of metal until it turns orange in color

- Place the piece of metal across the hardy, at the exact point you need to cut it

- Strike the piece of metal using a hammer and rotate the metal after every few strikes

- Stop hammering when about ¾ of an inch remains uncut. If you cut pieces of metal all the way through, you risk damaging your hardy and hammer. Additionally, your piece of metal may fly off and turn into a dangerous projectile

- Bend your piece of metal back and forth until the remaining part breaks

- Confirm if your cut is the way you intended it to be. If it is not, reheat the piece and cut it again

An assortment of hardy tools for different job descriptions

Fuller

If you need to create hollows and grooves on your piece of metal, the fuller is the perfect tool for the job. You can also use a fuller to produce rounded corners, give jagged edges a smooth finish, or spread a piece of metal. A fuller is designed in a two-piece format.

A fuller comes in a two-piece design

How to Use a Fuller

- Select the right fuller for the job according to the shape you need to create

- Take the bottom piece of the tool and fit it into the hardy hole

- Retrieve the hot piece of metal and place it on top of the fuller

- Take the second piece of the fuller and place it on top of the metal, sandwich style

- Use your hammer to strike the top piece of the fuller

- Hit the top fuller repeatedly until you acquire the desired shape

- Remove the piece of metal and observe if you have achieved your goal – reheat it if you have not and repeat the process

A fuller sandwiches a piece of metal and hammered to produce the desired results

Pritchel

As mentioned earlier, a pritchel is a tool used to bore holes in metal. Holes are created using a technique called punching or drifting, where the pritchel is hammered into a hot piece of metal.

A pritchel is used to punch holes in metal

Pritchel Usage

- Depending on the size of holes you want to punch, select the right-sized pritchel

- Heat your piece of metal until it is orange in color

- Use the tip of the pritchel and place it where you intend to punch a hole

- Strike the pritchel with your hammer to begin piercing the hole

- If you find it challenging to hold your piece of metal, hammer and pritchel at the same time, seek an extra pair of hands to assist you

- When the hole begins to punch through, place your piece of metal over the pritchel hole

- Turn your piece of metal to the flip side

- Strike the pritchel with your hammer until the hole pierces through

- The piece of metal that makes way for the punched hole will fall inside the pritchel hole

- Straighten your piece of metal if a bend has formed during the hammering process

- Asses the punched hole to ensure it is the required size. If it is not, reheat your piece of metal and pick a different-sized pritchel

A blacksmith using a pritchel to punch a hole on a horseshoe

Measuring Tools

In blacksmithing, measurements are an integral part of the craft because they ensure the size accuracy of your finished product. For example, if you receive an order for a wall hanging, you must measure the distance between the wall studs that will hold your item. Then, you need to ensure your final product matches the stud distance for a perfect fit.

Precise measurements can help you set the correct prices for your products. The size of a product is directly proportional to the amount of material it will use up. Based on that, you can estimate how much to charge or quote for a certain job, shielding you from making losses.

Also, if you make a product, somebody comes across it, likes it, and orders the same item, it becomes easier to duplicate the job if you keep track of measurements.

To achieve measurement accuracy, you require the right tools, which include;

Ruler

Blacksmiths prefer to use metal rulers in place of their wooden counterparts. Wooden tools, rulers included, should never be used in a workshop because you will be dealing with metals heated to extremely high temperatures. Wood, on the other hand, is a flammable material.

Use a ruler with both SI (metric) and Imperial measurements; the two systems combined are important as you can easily convert one to the other. A tape measure also adds value to your measuring tasks, especially the 16 feet (5 meters) long model made from flexible steel.

A metal hook ruler is ideal for the workshop. Avoid using wooden rulers at all costs.

Square

Often, you will find the need to bend pieces of metal. A square is a crucial tool that helps you get an accurate angle since it is impossible to assess angles visually.

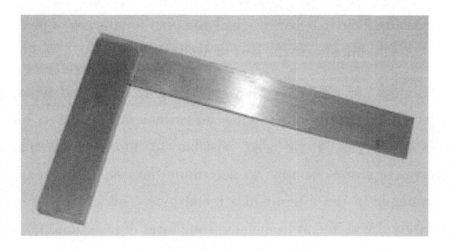

A blacksmith's square to accurately measure angles

The square should be held firmly on one end of a bent piece of metal so you can be able to determine the degree of adjustment required to realize the intended angle. Heat your piece of metal, adjust the bend, assess and measure your angle, and reheat the metal as dictated by the measure if necessary.

A quick hack is to place your piece of metal on the anvil's face placing the bend at the edge, pointing towards the direction of the ground. The metal should automatically form an angle of 90°.

Calipers

Calipers help you measure the thickness or external diameter of a round piece of metal. For example, if you need to measure a circular bar or a ball you plan to attach to a piece of metal, calipers are the best tools for the job.

Calipers are available in several designs, sizes, and types, including others with digital measurements displayed on LCD screens. It is also possible to measure internal diameters, for example, to determine the amount of space available in the interior of a metal pipe. This can come in handy if you intend to include some form of insertion into a pipe.

Calipers can measure the external and internal diameters of circular objects

How to Use Calipers

- Take both arms of your calipers and place them on either side of the item you are measuring

- Adjust the caliper so that it tightens on the object

- Observe and read the measurement at the tightest point

- This is the measure of each of the caliper's arm tips

- For an internal diameter, place both caliper arms on the inside of the metal you intend to measure on either side and note the reading

Chapter 3: Tongs, Vises, Hammers, Power Tools and Gear

Tongs

Tongs are essential tools in a blacksmith's workshop. Their main job is to protect your hands from the heat of the fire as you place or retrieve metals.

Also, they are like an extension of your hands, and you can use them to hold a piece of metal in place as you work on it on the anvil. If you choose to cool pieces of metal after retrieving them from the fire, you use tongs to dip them into the water.

Tongs consist of two identical metal pieces bound by a rivet at the fulcrum/pivot point. The part directly above the binding rivets is the handle, while the part located below the rivets is the jaw. Tongs are available in numerous shapes and sizes and varied jaw designs.

Some blacksmiths prefer to construct their own calipers and customize them depending on their frequently encountered work. Later, you will also attempt to create a personal pair.

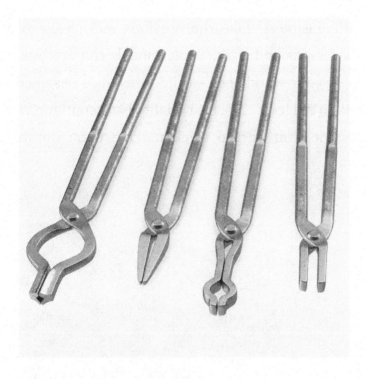

Some of the different types of tongs available

When using tongs, first consider the size of the metal piece you need to lift and pick a pair with the correct handle length. Always test the weight of your piece of metal first before lifting it completely. If the 'feel' is not comfortable, try out another pair of tongs.

Vise

A vise's main job is firmly holding a piece of metal in place while freeing your hands, allowing you to work on it. Once the metal is secured, you can hammer or twist it, and it will not shift positions. Like the previous tools, vises come in various designs and sizes. Some models can are mountable on top of your workbench, while others are designed to be fastened to the legs. The best quality blacksmithing vises are those made from forged steel, making them durable and hardy.

A blacksmith's vise mounted on an improvised work bench

Vice Usage Tips

Begin by considering the size of the piece of metal you intend to work on and use it to choose a suitable vice. If possible, avoid vises with textured jaws because they can add unwanted markings to your metal piece.

After sufficiently heating your metal piece, place it in the jaws of the vise with the heated part jutting out—exercise caution to avoid accidentally brushing against the hot protruding metal. Next, tighten the jaws of the vise until your piece of metal is firmly held. Then, you can begin working on it.

Hammers

Blacksmiths use a wide variety of hammers; they can weigh between 1-16 pounds (0.45-7.25kgs). However, most artisans prefer hammers that weigh 2-3 pounds (0.90-3.6kgs) because they are lighter and thus more comfortable to handle and swing.

The most popular hammers are;

- **Ball-peen hammer** – Also preferred by engineers, machinists, and mechanics, ball-peen hammers are ideal for thinning, shaping, and riveting metal

A ball-peen hammer, suitable for shaping, riveting and thinning pieces of metal

- **Cross-peen hammer** – designed with one end pointed, while the other is flat, this hammer is common in forging

A cross-peen hammer is ideal for forging

Hammer Usage Tips

Try out a few hammers by holding them in your hand to establish their weight. Choose a light one. A blacksmith swings a hammer a few hundred times a day; therefore, it is important to use a light and comfortable hammer that you can handle for long periods without straining. Also, consider how balanced the hammer feels in your hand and use the one that feels just right.

Avoid using carpenters' hammers; they are not built for blacksmithing, and also those with a textured head as they can deface your piece of metal.

When swinging your hammer, grip it lightly but firmly close to the end of the handle. The bottom part of your hammer's handle should protrude less than 1 inch (25mm) from your pinky finger. The movement of your swings should be controlled – do not put too much emphasis on strength; control is more important. Also, use your entire arm in the swing and ensure your elbow remains close by your side at all times.

Power Tools

A contemporary blacksmith's workshop usually has both modern and traditional tools. For example, it is common to find a workshop with power hammers alongside hand-held hammers or both a power drill and a manual drill side by side.

Power tools increase a blacksmith's productivity; you can do more in less time. Power tools also alleviate the muscle aches and strain associated with traditional tools. For example, if you skip swinging a hammer for an entire day and use a power hammer instead, you can work on larger metal pieces, at a faster rate and for extended hours.

Power Hammers

Power hammers have been around since the 1800s. The difference back then was that in the 1800s, power hammers used water power, which evolved over time to steam, electricity, and hydraulic to pneumatic (compressed air) systems.

Power hammers are built using a tall, narrow design equipped with a motor that supplies power to the hammer and a lever to control the speed and intensity of strikes.

An air-powered hammer

Even with a power hammer, a blacksmith still needs creativity and technical skills to shape metal; a power hammer on its own does not enable skills. Apart from saving you the energy of manually swinging a hammer, a power hammer does little else.

Grinders

Angle Grinder

This is a hand-help power tool designed with a pneumatic or electric motor that rotates a sand paper disk at high speeds of up to 10,000 Rotations per Minute (RPM). Once you switch on the grinder and the disk begins to spin, press it firmly onto the surface of the piece of metal you are working on. Here, ensure that you use both hands to ensure you can maintain a firm grip and apply pressure. Alternatively, you can secure your piece of metal using a vice to keep it from moving around.

An angle grinder with various grade disks

You can also use a grinder for any of the following tasks;

- Polish, grind, shape, buff, and sharpen metals

- Sharpen metal tool blades

- Smoothen rough edges or welded parts on metal

- Get rid of rust and metal flakes

Bench Grinder

The main difference between an angle and bench grinder is that the latter has brushes or grinding wheels that can be interchanged in place of a disk. Instead of taking the grinder to the metal, you take it to the grinder when using a bench grinder since it is a tabletop machine. Therefore, you need to hold your piece of metal firmly when working on it.

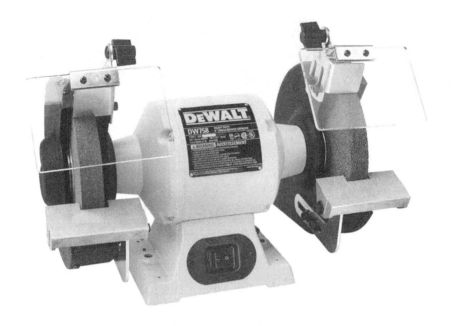

A table-top bench grinder

Like sandpaper, the different wheels and disks in grinders represent various grades for specific tasks. Before beginning a job, assess and determine the right wheel or disk to use.

Drills

Drills support drill bits that enable a blacksmith to bore round holes in metal. Bits are groove-filled spiraling thin pieces of metal and at the bottom of each bit is a small piece of metal that protrudes. This is what grips the metal as it is drilled into.

A set of drill bits that can pierce holes through metal

Bits offer various drilling options, and you can choose them according to the size of the hole(s) you want to drill – threaded or smoothened holes. Bits are inserted into a drill, and when the device is switched on, a motor rotates the bit, which can then pierce holes through metal when a little pressure is exerted.

A bit attached to a power drill

A blacksmith's workshop has the choice of either going for a hand-held or drill press. A hand-held drill requires manual pressure to bore holes in metal. On the other hand, a drill press lowers a spinning bit into the metal while it is clamped on the drill.

Blacksmithing Gear

Like any other craft, blacksmithing has its hazards associated with tools, high temperatures, and the physical nature of the job. However, adequate measures and the right gear reduce the risks posed to a minimum.

Every day before you leave for the workshop, keep in mind that what you wear and how you carry yourself can make a huge difference. For example, when choosing what shoes to wear, remember that if a tool drops, it gains momentum on its way down. Can your shoes protect you if a hammer accidentally falls from the work bench and onto your foot?

Clothing

Always go for fire and heat-resistant clothing capable of protecting you against flames, sparks, and high temperatures, which constitute a typical day in the office in a blacksmith's workshop. This can include clothing made from natural fibers, preferably woven tightly, such as wool, leather, and cotton. Natural fibers are fire and heat-resistant. Avoid fabrics such as nylon which can melt on your body.

Jackets, coveralls, and shop coats should be long-sleeved, while the pants you choose to wear should be long enough to cover the top of your boots and shoes. This keeps hot metal or coals from accidentally falling into your footwear. Shirts should also be long-sleeved and always tucked into your pants.

Boots are the ideal shoes for the workshop, preferably designed with rubber soles, light, high-top, and fitted with a steel toe guard. It's best to avoid synthetic shoes because they can easily melt if they come into contact with fire.

An example of an ideal blacksmith boot

Make it a habit to always don a cap, and if you have long hair, tie it at the back of your head. Bandanas can also act as good substitutes for caps.

Before you begin any task, go through your pockets and get rid of any flammable items, like a box of matches or a lighter. Also, double-check your clothes to ensure they do not have oil or other stains that can easily catch fire.

Remember that sparks and hot metal pieces are trappable in baggy clothing pockets, cuffs, and shirts with open necks;

avoid wearing any of them in the workshop. If you do not have coveralls at the onset, you can purchase old clothes from second-hand stores; but they should not be frayed or baggy. Remove any jewelry, including rings, before commencing any task.

Safety Equipment

Get into the habit of wearing a pair of approved blacksmithing glasses or goggles to shield your eyes from flying pieces of metal or sparks. The best types of glasses are those equipped with a side protection feature. Wear them when working with a wire brush, chipping, filing, or grinding.

Prescription safety glasses approved by the Occupational Safety and Health Administration (OSHA) are readily available for purchase on most safety gear websites and stores.

The best goggles for blacksmiths should have side protection as well

A blacksmith's ideal gloves are leather work type and made using Kevlar and cotton. They protect your hands from blisters, burns, and cuts from jagged metal pieces. Welding gloves can also offer the same protection. Before wearing your gloves, always inspect them to ensure they are not damaged, which can expose you to injury.

Gloves should be loose enough, and you should be able to shake them off at a moment's notice

Tight-fitting gloves are not recommended —you should be able to shake your pair off with ease if necessary. In case your gloves catch fire, never dip them in water because the resultant steam can burn your hands. Quality gloves should provide you with ample time to drop a hot object picked accidentally. It is best to wear protective gloves on both hands.

Excessive noise can make you feel fatigued and increase your chances of encountering an accident. Wearing ear protection keeps out the noise. Noise is measured in decibels (db), and prolonged exposure to loud noises of over 90 decibels can cause ear damage. When a hammer hits metal, the noise produced can reach 85db, while a power saw's noise levels can hit 110db.

Ear protection is important to shield your ears from damage from loud workshop noises

Chapter 4: Blacksmithing Metal

Let's simplify this:

What is Metal?

Metal is the main raw material used in blacksmithing and classified in Chemistry as a chemical element. An element refers to a substance that is impossible to break down into a simpler form through a chemical reaction.

Metals fall into two groups;

- **Ferrous** – those that contain iron

- **Non-ferrous** – alloys and all other metals that do not contain any iron content

Characteristics of Metal

Ductility – refers to a metal's ability to be transformed into wires or hammered to produce thin metal sheets.

Malleability – means metal can be bent or shaped without the risk of cracking or breaking.

When metal is at room temperature, except for mercury, it remains solid and can be fused or melted. Additionally, it does not allow light to pass through; it is opaque, but it can reflect light if polished. Also, metal is a good conductor of heat, electricity, and electropositive which means, it can form positive ions and lose electrons. It can also be combined with other metals to form alloys.

Metal is not only important to blacksmithing alone. Humans require small quantities of iron in their diets, such as zinc, sodium, calcium, potassium, magnesium, manganese, chromium, iron, and copper.

Production of Iron

Brief History of Iron in Blacksmithing

Iron is a naturally occurring element, but when mined from the depths of the earth, it does not initially appear in its natural form. It is first mixed with rock (ore) and then separated to produce iron in the form we are well familiar with. History shows that blacksmiths have used iron as their raw material since the Iron Age —around 1200-500 BC.

Separating the iron from ore is referred to as smelting. It takes place in a smelter. Coal or charcoal is the fuel used in smelters, and both have high carbon content. The chemical reaction that follows creates extremely high temperatures. The carbon produces carbon monoxide, which eliminates all the oxygen contained in the ore, leaving only metal. The reaction causes the ore to melt, and in the process, it forms slag, a waste product in solid form.

Before metal, blacksmiths used bronze for their craft largely because bronze has a lower melting point compared to iron; 1742° Fahrenheit (950° Centigrade), compared to Iron's 2786° Fahrenheit (1530°C) respectively. Back then, there was no way fires could burn hot enough to melt iron.

When it was discovered the secret to hotter fires was to increase oxygen levels, bellows were invented. This was the turning point that enabled the easier separation of iron from ore.

The Carbon Factor

Earlier, we mentioned coal and charcoal were used as fuel in smelters, and they contain high amounts of carbon, and when iron mixes with a non-metallic or metallic substance, it forms an alloy. Carbon is not a metal; its name comes from *carbo*, Latin for coal.

Carbon is the fourth most abundant element based on mass in the entire universe, and only hydrogen, helium, and oxygen precede it. Carbon is present and ranked second after oxygen in all life forms, including humans.

The carbon content in naturally occurring metal is extremely low by weight, at 0.05%. However, once it is included after the smelting process, iron is referred to as carbon steel or steel. Therefore, carbon steel is an alloy.

However, it is worth noting that the percentage of carbon directly affects the quality of iron. It determines how steel reacts to welding, heating, cooling, and hammering; for example, if metal-carbon percentage surpasses 1.7%, it will be almost impossible to work on. This also means high carbon content lowers the melting point of the metal. These are the factors that determine the best metal for blacksmithing.

Below is a breakdown of the carbon content contained in various metals.

Metal Type	Characteristics	Weight of carbon content	Uses
Mild, Medium, and High Carbon Steel	It is neither too soft nor too hard, and although it is strong, it is easy to shape. It does not crack or break in the process. Melting point - 2467°-2667° F (1353°-1464°C)	0.07-2% Carbon	Used by blacksmiths and is the best for beginners. It also makes structures in construction, machines, cars, and tools
Iron	Melting point 2786°F (1530°C)	0.05%	Practically very few uses
Cast Iron	Tough, breakable similar to glass, not easy to shape, and it melts at low temperatures	2-4% carbon content	Not used by blacksmiths but is melted and placed in molds or casts to produce

			pans, parts of machines, and pipes
Wrought Iron	Not strong like steel but can be welded, shaped, re-heated and re-shaped	0.25% and below	Currently not used much. Previously, it was used to produce bolts and nuts, gun barrels, knives, railings, and chains

Metal for Blacksmiths

In the past, blacksmiths used wrought iron to produce various artifacts. In old English, 'Wrought' translates to 'work.' So, wrought iron means 'work iron.' This was until the mid-1800s when steel replaced it. If you refer to the carbon content table above, you will observe that wrought iron contains a very low carbon percentage, making it a challenge to work with.

Today, carbon steel is the metal predominantly used, and although some blacksmiths still refer to it as wrought iron or iron, steel or carbon steel is the correct term and the one you should get used to using.

As illustrated in the table above, steel is available in mild, medium, and varieties of carbon content. Mild steel is the best first option for new blacksmiths because it is easier to shape and heat. Even if it is not heated to the correct temperature, you can still mold and shape it. Also, if you cool it in water, it does not crack.

Whenever you set out to purchase steel, inquire about its carbon content. If you are unsure about the metal you are about to start working on, undertake a simple exercise using a grinder. High carbon steel produces a lot of sparks, while mild carbon emits very few sparks.

Other Types of Blacksmithing Steels

The World Steel Association has classified over 3500 different steel grades, all differing in environmental, physical, and chemical properties. 75% of these steel varieties are quite recent and have emerged in the last 20 years.

Out of all the steel varieties available, how do you identify the right type of steel to purchase? According to the American Iron and Steel Institute, steel has four main groups;

63

Carbon Steel

We have already learned and established that this is the most popular variety of steel used by blacksmiths worldwide and the right one to use as you commence your blacksmithing journey.

Alloy Steel

Additional elements, or alloying elements, are added to metal to create alloys and influence the original metal properties. For example, it could be to make the metal resistant to corrosion, enable it to become wieldable, make it harder, and increase its ductility or formability. To improve its properties, elements such as titanium, aluminum, silicon, chromium, manganese, or copper are mixed with plain metal.

Alloy steel can be used in numerous ways, from flatware and hand tools to more demanding applications such as nuclear reactors, jet engines, and turbine blades. Also, alloy steels are used in transformers and electric motors because of their magnetic properties.

Stainless Steel

This is an alloy of iron and chromium with a 10.5% minimum. If chromium levels reach 11%, the steel becomes over 200 times more resistant to corrosion than other steels. A layer of chromium oxide is formed on steel when the two are merged; this merger is responsible for increased corrosion protection. Sometimes, Nickel is also added to increase resistance to corrosion, while molybdenum is used to enable formability, which ensures the metal can be molded without the risk of permanent damage.

Due to these unique features, stainless steel is used widely in various industries such as automotive, construction, and kitchen appliances.

Tool Steels

As the name suggests, tool steels are commonly used in tools. The alloying elements mostly used include vanadium, cobalt, tungsten, and molybdenum. The result is durable, hard, abrasion, deformation, and heat resistant steel.

Recycling Steel

As a beginner in blacksmithing, you may find buying steel to practice and learn the craft prohibitive, cost-wise. Additionally, this practical stage consists mainly of trial and error until you master the art, and most of the steel you use will probably go to waste.

To avoid buying steel until you are good at blacksmithing and can earn from your products, consider recycling steel, which is free and readily available. You will be surprised at the stuff people throw away.

A junkyard is a great place to source steel to recycle

The best place to begin your search is in scrap/junkyards, dumpsites, basements, and garages of friends and relatives.

Look out for items such as;

- Antique tools such as metal files

- Leaf springs and other springs of old model cars

- Metal drums, especially the 55 gallon

- Spikes from railroads

- Braided cables

- Rebar (reinforced steel used in construction)

- Lawnmower blades

Steel Grading System Explained

When you learn enough and feel ready to purchase steel for your workshop, there is one thing you will realize: the sheer amount of numbers used to identify steel. This is called the carbon steel grade system, a system used since the 1940s.

The numbers involved are four or five in total and the occasional alpha character to signify a unique characteristic. The first numbers in the grading system inform you of the general category the particular steel falls in and the alloys included;

- 1 – Indicates carbon steel

- 4 – Molybdenum

- 5 - Chromium

- 6 – Chrome vanadium

- 8 – Molybdenum, nickel, chromium

- 9 – Manganese and silicon

The second number indicates any additional elements that can influence the steel's properties.

The common number that appears here is usually zero, which means there are no additional elements. For example, if A1 appears second, it shows sulfur is included.

If other alloys are present, a letter appears after the second number;

- B – Boron, responsible for increased hardness

- L – Lead, which makes machinability possible

Finally, the last couple of numbers represent the carbon content percentage found in the specific steel –XX is equal to XX% steel. It is difficult to control the carbon content to a definite percentage during the steel manufacturing process. Therefore, the percentage that appears is theoretical.

For instance, if 1095 appears on steel;

- 1 – Indicates it is carbon steel

- 0 – No other alloys are present

- 95 – Refers to 0.9% to 1.0% carbon content

1095 blade steel

To begin blacksmithing on the right footing, steels that fall somewhere in between 1050 to 1095 are the best for you because they are softer compared to tool steels and will not damage your tools, like your beginner's grinder or drill.

But your choice of steel may also depend on other factors and circumstances such as the project you are undertaking, the workshop set up, tools available, among others.

The best approach is to keep an open mind and experiment as much as possible until you identify the steel that works best for you under the prevailing conditions.

Chapter 5: The Forge

In its original form, metal is too hard to work on —unless it is heated. Blacksmiths use a forge that produces extremely high heat temperatures to enable the heating process to soften the metal at hand. A forge is a type of hearth made up of a basin-like structure, a source of heat and oxygen supply. Once the metal is hot and soft, it can be molded to create various artifacts.

Blacksmiths have used forges for centuries, and although designs and fuels have changed over the years, the basic concept of the forge remains the same. Today, forges are classified depending on the fuel that powers them;

- Solid fuels such as coal, coke, charcoal, and peat run traditional forges

- The modern-day forge versions fuelled by natural gas or propane

Surprisingly, traditional forges are still active to this day — you can DIY one to save costs.

Traditional Forge

As indicated earlier, peat, industrial coke, and charcoal fueled —and fuel— the traditional forge. They may have different designs, and sizes may also vary, but they operate similarly. A traditional forge resembles a conventional fireplace, and its design allows metals to be heated and transformed into a malleable state.

Traditional forge fires are controlled in three ways;

- Decreasing or increasing the amount of oxygen/air

- Through the shape of the preferred fuel

- According to the volumes of fuel introduced

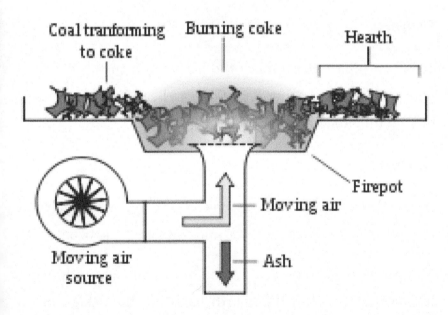

A basic illustration of a traditional forge

Although the different parts of the traditional forge have evolved in one way or another, the basic features of this age-old forge include;

Hearth

This is where the actual fire burns, heating of metal occurs, and the control center for the fire's intensity. Stone, fired brick, and mud-brick are the most common materials used to construct the hearth. Some traditional forges that emerged later use iron.

Tuyere

This is a pipe that supplies the air/oxygen to the fire. It is designed so that the amount of air can be reduced, increased, or shut off altogether.

Bellows

Also called a blower, bellows make it possible to force air into the tuyere to increase pressure and the size of the fire.

To operate the fire in a traditional forge, a blacksmith places his preferred fuel in the hearth based on the design of the forge. Moving air is then introduced with the bellows as the source. Bellows work using the same principle as fans, and the air produced is channeled through the tuyere. With increased amounts of air, fuel is consumed faster – and the result is a hotter blazing fire.

Depending on the type of metal to be heated and the task at hand, a blacksmith balances air and fuel to suit the specific work and meet the workpieces' temperature requirements.

In classic coal-fuelled forges, the center of a flat hearth has the firepot where the actual fire will burn. The tuyere gains access to the fire from the bottom part of the hearth. When burning, the core will be a ball of fire above and in the firepot. At the heart of the fire, a layer of hot, not burning, coke forms a layer around it.

Traditional forges built indoors must be equipped with a vent and chimney to keep the smoke produced out of the workshop.

How to Build A Traditional Forge

Building your own traditional forge fuelled by charcoal is a great introductory way to grasp the basics of forging metal. This DIY project is easy to build, practical, and inexpensive. This DIY forge can reach the high temperatures required to heat any metal.

Materials Required

- A circular, square, or rectangular container preferably made from stainless steel. This can range from an old barbeque grill, unused tank to a brake drum

- Four M6 40mm bolts and their washers

- Air supply steel pipe

- Plaster of Paris

- Kiln, beach, or clean play sand

- Power drill and drill bit – 6mm

- Source of air pressure – air compressor, hand-crank blower or bellow

- Charcoal as the fuel

Step 1

Clear the area you intend to set up your forge; if possible, an outdoor space. Indoors is also possible, but it has to be a well-ventilated room. This prevents the build-up of carbon monoxide, a highly poisonous gas.

If it is in your garage, leave the doors open; and if it is your designated workshop, make provisions for an exhaust outlet, like a chimney or hood. You can also install a carbon monoxide detector device that monitors and warns you if the gas' levels get out of hand.

Prep yourself as well by wearing the necessary protective gear. At a minimum, you should have natural fiber clothing such as a coverall or long-sleeved shirt, gloves, and safety glasses.

Step 2

Place your container upside down and mark all four corners with small indentations using a punch or chisel. Take your power drill, 6mm bit, and drill four holes where you had previously marked.

You can use an old electric grill like this one to build a traditional forge.

Step 3

Insert your four 40mm M6 bolts through each hole and fix their respective washers and bolts tightly. This raises your forge from the ground and doubles up as insulation. This is if the container has no stand of its own.

Step 4

Pick one side of your container and drill a hole to host your air supply pipe. Make sure your pipe extends around 6 inches away from the forge once inserted. This represents your tuyere to bring in oxygen for the forge fire.

The logic behind placing the air supply on the side is to ensure the practicality of your forge and ease of use. A tuyere placed at the bottom, for instance, will constantly fill with ash.

Step 5

Now, turn your attention to the air supply and attach your source to the tuyere you inserted earlier. Bellow, air compressor, or hand crank blowers are all ideal. Some innovative blacksmiths even use hair dryers. The only challenge with hairdryers is their limited settings, making it difficult to control oxygen amounts going into the forge.

Insert the air supply pipe into the container

Step 6

Mix your plaster of Paris with sand in a ratio of 50:50 and add a small amount of water to create a mixture that resembles clay. The idea is to evenly spread a 1cm layer of the mixture around the inside of your forge container. The purpose of the plaster is to provide a coating layer to enable refraction and insulate the base of your container. After completion, give the mixture an allowance of a few hours to dry.

Coat the inside of the container with plaster of Paris for insulation and refraction purposes.

Step 7

After the coating dries, fuel your forge, light it up and switch on your air supply to fan the fire.

A completed DIY traditional forge

Traditional Forge Usage Tips

To get the fire burning quickly, begin by cleaning the firepot. Then, form a ball with some old newspapers and light them. Take your fuel of choice, add, and open the tuyere to activate the air supply. Ensure to slowly form a mound on the firepot located at the center of the forge. Around the fire, place more fuel and rake any fuel that may have fallen outside the mound back to the center while increasing the amount of fresh fuel around the fire.

Poke and move the fuel around in the firepot while increasing the oxygen supply to increase the temperature. Have a can of water or open tank conveniently placed within easy reach to cool the fire when it burns too hot. Keep an eye on the fire's progress, and when it is hot enough, place your steel into the coal horizontally at an angle slightly less than 45°.

Place the steel approximately 2 inches (5cm) under the coal or charcoal. If you place your piece of metal on top of the fire, it will not heat up as it should. Place only one metal into the fire at a time for better results.

Drawbacks of the Traditional Forge

- A fire can stubbornly refuse to start sometimes and take a huge chunk of your time to get it going, especially when using coal or charcoal

- Finding traditional fuels can be difficult now that the world is turning more to clean fuels. Remember, a forge does not use conventional charcoal, like the one used in barbeques. Charcoal for forging is sold as natural lump charcoal. The difference is that natural lump charcoal emits huge amounts of carbon important for the forging process

- Traditional forges built in a workshop can take up too much space

- A traditional forge fire requires constant attention. A moment of distraction can lead to the fire fizzling out

Propane/Gas Forges

Gas and propane forges are the modern and upgraded versions of the traditional forge and are highly recommended for beginners because they are easy to use and portable; all you need is to fuel the forge and light it. However, experienced blacksmiths suggest always having an extra fuel tank on standby, especially when working on large projects because gas and propane forges tend to burn fuel faster than traditional forges. Gas and propane forges are also commercially available in various designs, sizes, and prices.

Most gas and propane forges' benefits depend on the type of fuel used. Gas and propane are both clean and green energies. Clean because they do not produce any residue such as ash or soot when they burn; green since they are environmentally friendly. Their portability means you can work anywhere and on any kind of project.

A gas forge burner

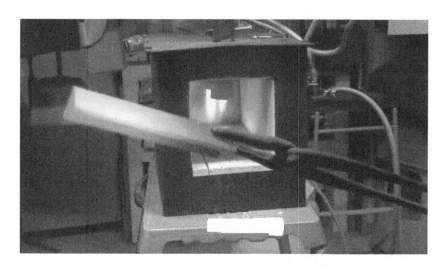

A propane-powered forge at work

Things to Consider When Buying a Gas/Propane Forge

The hearth where metal is heated is the most important part of a forge and your key consideration when shopping for gas or propane forges. It must be effective, safe, and user-friendly to beginners and established blacksmiths.

Additionally, it's best to get a forge built from durable material that can withstand high temperatures over a long period without falling apart. If possible, settle for a forge constructed with alumina, silica, and zirconium; they can handle the most extreme heat.

The weight and size are also key considerations to ease your working mode. Airflow, fuel consumption rate, and temperature control features are also vital.

Choose a gas forge depending on the blacksmithing tasks you intend to take up. Some forges are designed for niche tasks. For example, some are dedicated to jewelers, others for knives and swords (blade smiths), while others are made for general blacksmithing.

Size

Size is an important consideration, and the answer to the best size to choose lies in the type of blacksmithing you plan to venture into. If you intend to produce small objects like jewelry or pocket knives, a crucible-style forge will cater to your needs. On the other hand, you can comfortably create mid-sized items using a 7-9 inch gas forge. Larger and longer objects require additional space and a bigger 40-50 inch gas forge.

The secret is to try and determine, beforehand, the largest objects you may forge. It is a tough decision. Another safer approach is to purchase a gas forge that can handle both small and large items instead of upgrading later, which is expensive.

Fuel consumption

The performance of a gas forge determines how much gas or propane it consumes. For example, if you use the standard range of 15 to 20 pounds per square inch (PSI) of propane gas, you will probably get a runtime of between 4 to 7 hours — assuming you are using a 20-pound propane tank, which is the standard norm. If you can manage to lower your pressure while working, expect the runtime to increase by a significant margin.

However, if you upgrade to forges with multiple burners (2, 3, 4, or 5), the time estimate above is divided among the different burners according to their use. However, most blacksmiths who opt for multiple burner forges prefer the 100-pound propane tank over the 20-pound.

Forge Purpose

Some gas forges are built for casting, while others are for blacksmithing. Casting is when metal is heated to a semi-liquid form and then poured into casts to form products such as vases. Therefore, ensure you do not purchase a casting instead of a blacksmithing forge. A casting forge comes with a distinct feature – a casting cup, while blacksmithing forges are designed with an open space to place metal.

DIY Gas Forge

It is also possible to build a gas or propane forge. In fact, it is far much cheaper. However, guaranteeing safety and efficiency is a different story. As a beginner, it is highly recommended that you initially purchase a ready-made gas or propane forge.

Later, equipped with experience and skill, you can build your own. Even on a modest budget, you can find a suitable gas/propane forge to launch you —or a second-hand forge in good condition.

Chapter 6: Forging and Techniques Used

Let's dive right in:

Hot Forging

As we have discovered, forging is the process of shaping heated metal to a desired shape using compressive forces, such as hammering. Hot forging is the blacksmithing term used to describe the act of hammering a piece of heated metal placed on an anvil until it forms an envisioned shape. The heat from the forge is responsible for softening the metal and enabling it to be worked on without cracking or breaking.

A blacksmith hot forging a piece of metal

When metal is heated to its respective forging temperature, it transforms and becomes as soft as clay, allowing a blacksmith to create various products. Forging processes are classified according to the temperatures required to achieve molding. These are;

- Cold forging – where metal is soft when cold and does not require heating

- Warm forging – metal is heated slightly and forged

- Hot forging – metal is heated to high temperatures to enable molding

As a beginner, the most important process worth mastering is hot forging, which is most commonly practiced and lays the foundation for the other processes.

On the other hand, a forge is the heating equipment used to heat the metal.

Temperature and Color

If you have seen various images that capture blacksmiths working, you will realize the workshops they work in are all dimly lit. This is intentional and by design. The low lighting enables a blacksmith to closely observe a piece of metal in the forge and discern when it reaches its forging temperature.

As the forge's temperature rises, the piece of iron temporarily changes color from black – blue – purple – red – orange – yellow to white. When it changes to yellow, it is ready for molding, and the temperature at this point could be between 1832 – 2300°F (1000-1260°C). To get the scope of the high temperatures, remember water boils at 100°C (212° F). The colors reverse in the same order as the metal cools.

The maximum temperature a piece of metal should be heated is 2400°F (1316°C); this is the point it turns white. Immediately after your piece of metal touches the vise or anvil, it begins to cool at a fast rate, which gives you a limited window to work on it.

Closely watch the color as you work and if you have not completed forging the metal by the time it changes to light red, return it into the forge to heat up again. Repeat this process until you have forged your piece of metal to the desired shape.

Metal Heating Tips

When creating a certain product for the first time, keep track of the time your piece of metal takes to reach its forging temperature. This makes it easier if you need to reproduce the same item again. Always watch your piece of metal while it is in the forge, taking note of the various color changes because over or under heating may mess up your final result. Remember, metal pieces with a large surface area or thinner ones will attain their respective forging temperatures faster.

Molding temperatures vary from metal to metal; also, it depends on your source of fuel, type of project, and kind of forge in use.

Before retrieving your piece of metal from the forge, make sure it is heated evenly and keenly observe its color; for most projects, a bright-orange to yellow color is usually suitable.

Carefully place your metal on the anvil or vise, and closely observe the movement of your piece as you hammer it. If your strikes are not changing the shape of the piece of metal, it could signal it needs additional heating.

The color your metal needs to achieve for you to work on it depends on a host of variables, such as the type of iron you are using to your preferred techniques. Despite this, here are general guidelines you can refer to;

- Red color – this is an indication that your piece of metal requires reheating

- Orange – in most metals, this is an ideal color to begin working on the metal

- Yellow – this is also a suitable color to retrieve your piece of metal and commence shaping it

Most aspiring blacksmiths make two common mistakes which you should strive to avoid;

- Retrieve a piece of metal before it is ready. Learn to exercise patience and give the metal sufficient time

- Keep hammering even when the metal has cooled and should be returned to the forge for reheating

Forging Techniques

Here are the various forging techniques you will need to master:

Outline

Blacksmithing techniques and tools have been developed over a long time, and this section covers all the basic and most important techniques. However, it is worth noting that sometimes, you may use more than one technique on one piece of metal depending on the item you intend to create.

Secondly, it may not be practically possible to use all the techniques mentioned.

You may also find that a certain technique has several other names. The most important thing to understand as a beginner is the steps involved in a specific technique and the expected outcome of the entire process. Gradually, you will discover that you can also use several other techniques to achieve a specific final result.

Generally, it is worth remembering that forging iron alters the shape and size of a piece of metal. However, the volume remains the same unless you cut off a piece of it. Therefore, if a piece of metal is shortened, it becomes thicker, while when flattened, it becomes longer or wider.

Upsetting

When you want o increase or decrease the diameter of a piece of metal, you will use a technique called upsetting. Since the volume will remain constant, your piece of metal can only get thicker.

In blacksmithing, upsetting is commonly used when you need to create a flat end on one or both sides of a piece of metal – such as a circular ball or a nail head.

Upsetting Process

Upsetting requires your piece of metal to be heated to above normal temperatures – until the metal is yellow to white. You should only heat the part of the metal you intend to reshape. Due to the extremely high temperatures and hammering, your piece of metal may bend somewhere you did not intend it to bend. One way to keep this from happening is to cool off the area below the end you plan to upset with water.

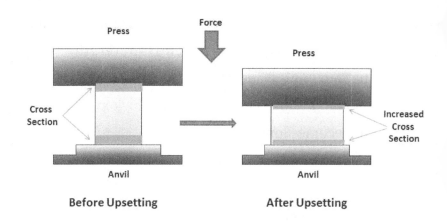

The upsetting process illustrated

Next, place your piece of metal on the anvil and ensure the heated end sticks out at the edge of the anvil. To avoid loose pieces of metal flying around, hold your piece of metal firmly. Grab your hammer and begin hitting the hot end while rotating the metal about a quarter turn after each square strike.

Keenly watch the color of your piece of metal and return it into the forge when it turns red and repeat the hammering process until you realize the required shape. If your metal has experienced a bend in the wrong places, straighten it out using your hammer.

Alternatively, you can place your hot piece of metal in a vertical position on your anvil and hammer it into shape. You can also clamp it on a vise with the heated end protruding outward but double-check to ensure the vise's jaws are tightly holding it before beginning to hammer.

Drawing Out

If the product you are working on demands your piece of metal should have a decreased diameter, and the length increased, drawing out is the forging technique that can achieve this. Diameter refers to the thickness or width of an object.

Since your piece of metal will not be cut off, it will maintain its original volume. This also means your piece will become thinner.

Drawing Out Tips

In the drawing out technique, heat your piece of metal until it is orange in color. Retrieve it and carefully place it in a flat position on the face of your anvil. Use the peen side of a hammer and strike the metal's surface squarely. After every few hammer strikes, rotate your piece of metal around 90° to ensure your piece does not end up flat and wide in shape.

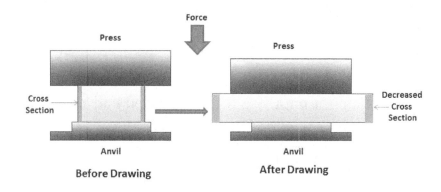

The drawing out process explained

Your hammering should be controlled and light to enhance strike accuracy; forceful strikes are rarely precise. By your 6th strike, you should notice the metal beginning to change shape.

Begin your strikes at the end of your piece of metal and push it towards your hammer as you proceed to shape the iron. Hammer along the length of your metal until you achieve the thickness and shape you want. Assess your progress and make the necessary adjustments.

If you need to reheat your piece of metal, watch it closely once it is back in the forge because thin metal can melt very fast.

Sharpening/Tapering

This technique is slightly similar to drawing out as you decrease the diameter and increase the length of your piece of metal. The difference is in sharpening/tapering; the process goes a step further to create a pointed or tapered end.

Sharpening/Tapering Process

The ideal metal shape to begin with is a squared piece that you should heat until it is orange in color. Once you achieve this, retrieve your piece from the forge and lay it on the anvil at a 45°angle.

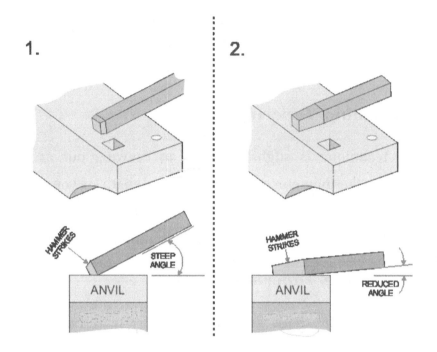

The step by step process of sharpening/tapering

Take your hammer and strike the piece squarely using the flat side of the tool and after every few hits, rotate it slowly at a 90° angle until you have a pointed sharp edge. Reheat your piece of metal if necessary and hammer it again until you achieve the desired results.

Twisting and Bending

You can use several techniques to twist or bend a piece of metal. One such technique is to use the horn of an anvil and hammer your piece until it twists or bends. Another method is to grip it on a vise or insert it into the hardy hole and use a bending tool to work on the piece of metal.

Twisting and Bending Tips

If you choose to use a bending tool —the two-pronged tool— place it inside the anvil's hardy hole with the prongs facing upwards. Remove your hot piece of metal, place it between the two prongs of the tool, and apply sufficient pressure to bend it.

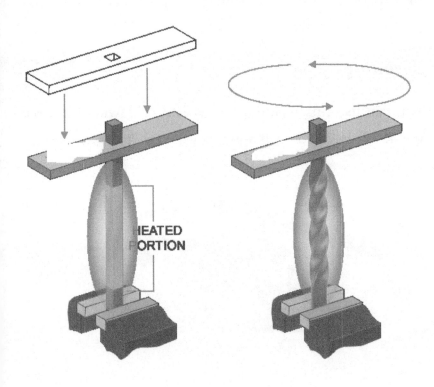

You can use a vise to hold the piece of metal you intend to twist, as illustrated above

With a vise, on the other hand, heat only the part of the metal you need to work on and grip it using the vise. The vise's jaws should hold the cool side of the metal tightly, leaving the hot end jutting out. Select a tool that you can use to provide leverage and bend or twist the metal. Proceed to bend or twist the metal to the shape you want.

Do not forget to use measuring tools such as a square — where needed— to create a right angle with the bend. To twist or bend, use tongs and exert pressure on one end of your piece of metal.

Scrolling

You can use this technique to create coils where a piece of metal rolls around itself and forms a loose or tight scroll.

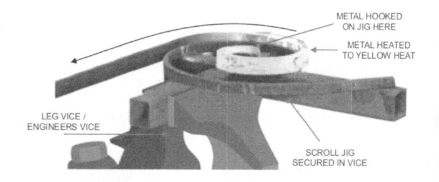

Scrolling Process

Heat your piece of metal until it is orange in color and carefully place it on the anvil's horn. Hammer it until it begins to curve around the horn, creating a bend in the process.

Next, lay your piece on the flat side of the anvil with the curved part facing upwards and strike the bend until it begins to coil around itself. Reheat in case it cools before completing the scroll and repeating the same process.

Riveting

Riveting is the process of joining two metal pieces. A good example is the two pieces of metal that create tongs. A rivet that joins metal together resembles a peg, metal pin, or a thick nail minus the pointed side.

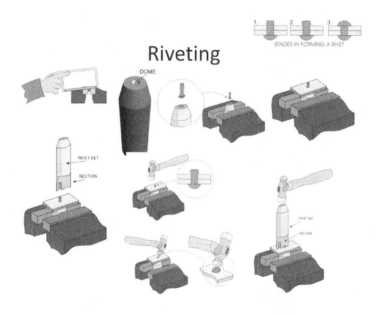

The riveting process explained in diagrams

<u>The Riveting Process</u>

Take the two pieces of iron you intend to join together and drill two identical holes in each piece at the point you want to join them. Line up the two holes and find a rivet that fits. Heat the rivet, and using the tongs, insert it into the two lined up holes. Using the upsetting technique, strike one of the flat ends of the rivet to create a head that will prevent the rivet from slipping off.

When the rivet cools down, it will contract and pull the two joined pieces of metal tightly together.

Forge Welding

This technique permanently attaches two pieces of metal using a forge. Forge welding results in the molecules of the two joined pieces of metal aligning to create a seamless and a single strong piece of metal without seams or joints. An example is a linked chain that forms one piece of metal that is continuous.

Forge Welding Process

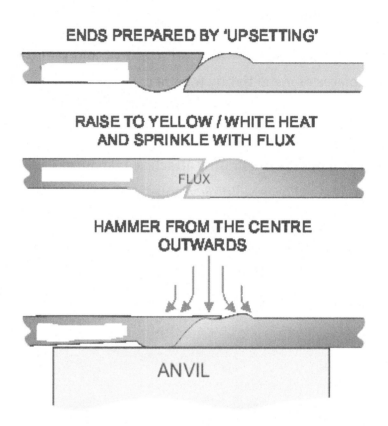

The forge welding process

The best metal for this technique is medium or high carbon steel. Heat your pieces of metal to a light yellow or white color; there is a strong possibility of sparks. After attaining the required temperatures, apply flux on the heated metal, such as Borax.

Flux is a substance that aids metal to merge, gets rid of any impurities, and impedes oxidation. On the other hand, Borax is an ore of boron in the form of a white crystalline solid. It is commonly used as a preservative, cleaning agent, and water softener.

Join the two pieces of metal together and use a hammer to strike them until they firmly stick to each other.

Chapter 7: Finishing Treatment and Workshop Safety

A glimpse at a piece of metal under a microscope reveals that it has crystal structures arranged in a series. Upon heating or melting metal, the crystals change in terms of their arrangement, which is the same story when metal cools: the crystals rearrange again. This change in a metal's crystals makes it harder and tougher.

Also, every time you work on metal —shaped, stretched, hammered, or flattened— the constituent crystals are compressed in the process. The result is less flexible and harder metal which becomes difficult to work on and mold.

Metal can undergo a finishing process that alters its features and original structure but does not affect the metal's shape. This is referred to as heat treatment. Metal is heated to a specific high temperature and then cooled. Heat treatment is a complex process that requires lots of practice to get right, as it demands pinpoint precision. One of the best metals for heat treatment is steel because it responds very well.

The type of heat treatment you choose to administer to your finished product depends on the features and structure you want your product to have – either to make it harder or softer.

- Heat tempering is often used to soften metal, decrease hardness and strength, restore ductility, increase toughness levels and eradicate stresses

- To transform your finished product into wear-resistant coupled with increased strength, hardening heat treatment is the way to go

To achieve the required results, it is extremely important to execute the right heating and cooling process for the specific type of metal you are using.

Heat Treatment Process

Generally, metal is heated to a specific temperature, which affects how the finished product will turn out. The temperature is then kept constant for a fixed duration; the length of time determines the features and structure the item will adopt.

The metal is then cooled, and the method used here also governs how the end product will end up.

- If the metal is cooled quickly, like in water, it becomes brittle and hard

- A slow cooling process, such as through cooled air, makes the metal soft

Hardening Heat Treatment

After finishing your product, you can embark on treatment to harden it to make your piece more durable. Hardening treatment involves quenching a heated piece of metal in water. Quenching refers to dipping the entire metal piece in water at room temperature. This treatment ensures your product is tough, hard, breakable, and brittle.

<u>The Treatment</u>

Once you have created your product, place it in the forge to heat until it changes to a dull cherry red color. The heating process ensures your piece is evenly heated at a slow pace, and you need to be vigilant so that it does not overheat.

Turn the piece over from time to time to achieve heat uniformity, only remove it after it has been in the forge for some time and heated at a constant temperature.

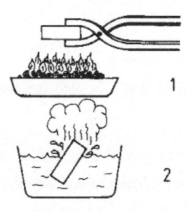

Hardening treatment

After retrieving your piece, dunk it into a large water tub, which we call quenching. The water should be at room temperature, and you should place your piece vertically into the tub. Once it is inside the water, quickly stir it.

You can also use other liquids such as oil in place of water, but since water is readily available, it is usually the better option.

Tempering Heat Treatment

This process comes after the hardening process described above.

The main objective of tempering is to reduce the metal's tension created by the hardening treatment and soften the brittle metal. After tempering, the final product will be tough, ductile, resilient, and malleable. It will still be tough and hard but soft enough to absorb strikes and handle pressure without shattering, breaking, or cracking.

A tempered piece of metal is also easier to file, cut, and shape.

It is worth noting that hardening creates a harder piece of metal than necessary. Therefore, tempering will not in any way affect or spoil your finished product.

Tempering Process

Retrieve your cooled-down piece of metal from the water tub after hardening and place it back in the forge for another round of heating; again, to a dull cherry red color. Let it remain there for a specific duration depending on the fire conditions.

Now remove it from the forge fire, set it down on the anvil, and allow it to cool until it is black. Next, place your piece in an insulated Perlite container overnight or place it somewhere in the workshop to cool down at room temperature. Avoid using a fan or any other cooling device.

Perlite is a natural volcanic glass, light in weight, containing high levels of water content.

Corrosion Prevention

There is a reason why iron ore is mined from the depths of the earth and not found on the earth's surface. It's because if iron is exposed to air and water, it tends to break down very fast. A piece of iron left exposed to the elements would eventually disintegrate and vanish.

After working so hard on your product, the last thing you want to see is the item being eaten away by corrosion. You can use some methods to protect your finished product from corrosion. Even if it is an item to be kept indoors, you still need to protect it from the humidity present in the air.

Protection Considerations

To ensure that you settle on the right protective measures, there are a few things you need to consider;

- Where will your finished product be displayed? Indoors or outdoors?

- Will it be used for food? If the answer is in the affirmative, you can only use a non-toxic finish

- What color would you like your item to be?

- Would you prefer a dull or shiny finish?

Metal Preparation

Using a grinder or wire brush, clean the surface of your product and the face of your anvil to get rid of carbon flakes. Next, decide on the best corrosion protection for your product based on how you answered the above questions.

Linseed Oil

Linseed oil provides a layer of rust-free protection for your product and leaves a dull black finish.

A piece of metal after receiving linseed oil treatment

Heat your piece of metal until it attains a black color. Remove it from the forge and place it on the anvil. Apply linseed oil all over the surface of your product with a piece of cloth or brush. Remember, the linseed oil is applied while the metal is still hot, so work carefully.

Beeswax

Beeswax protects your product against rust, but it is not weather-proof. It leaves a shiny black finish.

Bolts after beeswax application

Heat your product to black, place it on the anvil and rub the melted wax using a piece of cloth. The wax will probably melt since the metal will still be hot, but some will stick to it. If you want your product to shine more, use a cotton cloth to buff it after applying the wax.

Varnish

Varnish leaves a transparent and shiny finish layer on your piece of metal that protects against rust.

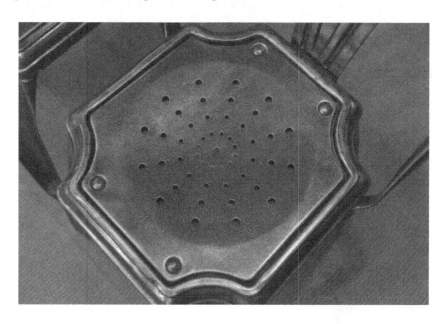

A steel chair after a coat of satin varnish finish is applied

This time, your product does not require heating. Varnish is applied to metal at room temperature using a brush. Varnish produces a strong, pungent vapor, and you need to wear a mask or work outdoors to prevent inhalation.

Paint

You can either choose to apply a colored or clear rust-resistant paint.

A piece of metal is painted using a brush

Use a sprayer or brush to apply the paint evenly on your finished product at room temperature. Work outdoors or wear a mask to avoid inhaling the strong fumes from the paint.

Workshop Safety

Every work environment, hobby, or sport comes with unique risks – including blacksmithing. Therefore, failing to observe safety practices can lead to serious or life-threatening injuries for you and others around you.

Blacksmiths are exposed to extremely high forge and metal temperatures, spatter flames, and sparks that can cause scalds and burns. The grinding or chipping of metal can produce shards, flying metal pieces and expose you to sharp metal edges.

Gas and propane forges are equipped with gases under high pressure that can explode if not handled properly, while power and hand tools pose various injury risks. Some chemicals used in blacksmithing may also emit toxic fumes that can place you in danger.

However, observing safety protocols can significantly reduce or eliminate the involved risks, despite all the potential dangers.

Safety Tips

Remain Alert

Always enter a workshop when you are well-rested and can concentrate on your planned tasks. Never touch any equipment, tools, or chemicals if you are under the influence of alcohol, drugs, or prescription medicine that causes drowsiness. Also, never smoke or allow anybody else to smoke inside the workshop.

Carefully inspect each tool or equipment before you start using it, and always be vigilant when it comes to the movement of others in the workshop. Make it a point to find out where the First Aid Kit, fire extinguisher, and emergency exits are.

Stay Hydrated

When the amount of water leaving your body is more than your intake, dehydration occurs, and signs include a dry mouth, reduced sweating, lightheadedness, nausea, muscle cramps, and thirst. Due to frequently working with the extreme temperatures of the forge and metal in an enclosed area, a blacksmith's risk of dehydration is high.

Therefore, always have a water bottle around to sip as you work.

Adhere to the Rules

Strictly follow all workshop rules and read through manuals using any equipment, tools, or chemicals. Additionally, wear appropriate protective gear and clothing for the task at hand. When learning the craft, pay heed to what your instructor says and follow the given directions to the letter.

Make sure you learn the various warning symbols placed around the workshop and contained in product labels, like those indicating compressed gases, flammable, explosive, or combustible materials.

Workplace Organization

Ensure you store your tools in a designated area, and after your day is over, return all of them to their proper place. Before beginning any task, clear your work area to eliminate hazards such as explosives, volatile, or flammable materials: store gas and propane cylinders in a separate, safe, and secure area.

Remove any clutter from your work area and clean it daily. Also, clean and clear the floor around; this ensures an efficient and safe working environment. Your work area should also be well-ventilated – open windows or use a fan. If possible, work outdoors whenever possible.

Planning

Mentally go through all the steps you need to complete a task before beginning. Plan until the final stage of each project. For example, the finishing treatment you will carry out to the corrosion prevention you intend to apply.

Lastly, never walk around with a hot piece of metal in hand.

Chapter 8: Blacksmithing Practice Projects for Beginners

Before you embark on your first blacksmithing project, it is important to test your skills on a few basic tasks.

Begin by attempting to forge a piece of metal, observe and identify the various color changes. In the process, practice how to rotate the metal while it is still in the forge so that it is evenly heated. You can also try out the different forging techniques explained earlier. For example, upsetting and tapering are beginner-friendly and frequently used methods used in blacksmithing.

Personal Assessment

To select a suitable project that you will manage to see through to completion, always try to establish the following beforehand;

- Which techniques will be required to finish the project successfully?

- What level of skill is required?

- Am I confident enough with my skills to take on this project?

- How challenging will the project be?

- How much time will it take me to complete the project?

Work order

To make it easier to complete a project, always outline the steps you need to go through before you begin —this will guide you along the way;

- Make a list of all the tools required

- Another list for the materials you will use includes the type, diameter, and length of the metal

- If you intend to replicate an existing completed piece, take measurements and record them

- If it is your creation you plan to produce, make a sketch on a piece of paper including all the dimensions

- List the first to the last step of the project to act as a reference point

- Make a list of the techniques the project demands in the order you will execute them

Templates

As you gain experience, it will reach a point where you need to design templates. These are forms of a project you are about to begin. You can design templates using metal, cardboard, or wood, and they provide a pattern that will assist and guide your project.

You will find templates helpful when;

- A previous project needs to be repeated

- You need to make numerous pieces that are exactly the same, such as tongs where both pieces are identical

- You require a visual guide on how a shaped piece of metal should resemble

- Working on a complex piece to provide guidance

- You design a prototype that you intend to improve with time

Templates are also vital if you work with a team because you can present your idea visually; receive instant feedback and practical suggestions on techniques, design, and materials.

Project 1: J-Hook

A J-hook is one of the most basic items a blacksmithing learner can begin with; it combines punching, tapering, twisting, and bending skills.

Step 1

Heat your piece of metal in the forge to its required molding temperature. Once done, attach a faceplate to your anvil and then place the red-hot metal on the edge at an angle of around 10° to create a shoulder. Slowly raise your piece of metal until it is level and hit the edges with consistent, measured, and overlapping strikes to flatten it.

Heat your piece to its forging temperature

Step 2

Turn your piece of metal to a 90° angle and hammer the shoulder's sides. Use a flat edge hammer so that you can square off your piece. If your piece bends, hammer it at its highest point so that it flattens.

Step 3

By now, your piece of metal is below its forging temperature. Return it to the forge, and before retrieving it, attach a faceplate on the anvil. Hold the heated metal firmly on the anvil with a punching tool. Hammer the tool on one side until it is ¾ through the metal. Repeat this process on the opposite side and expand the hole to the size you want to have on the hook. Next, bore through the hole on the faceplate.

Step 4

Relocate your piece of metal to the edge of the anvil that is farthest from you with the tip on the anvil's face. Lift the piece around an inch and hammer it with angled strikes. After each hit, rotate your piece 90° until you have the tip tapered 1/16 inch. To ensure uniformity, rotate the metal 180° after every six to eight strikes.

Use the tip of the anvil to shape the hook of your piece

Step 5

Return your piece to the forge for reheating. Once you remove it, place it over the edge of the anvil about ½ an inch. Gently hammer the pointed tip until it forms an L-shape. Rotate your metal's tip 180°so that its tip points upwards. Hammer the tip in the general direction of your body so that it curls. Once you have achieved this, quench your piece of metal in water to cool it.

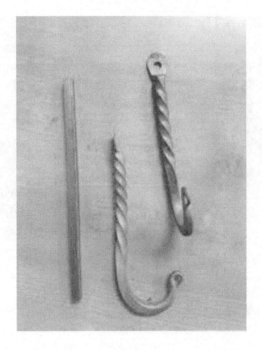

Hammer your piece to an L-shape

Step 6

Put your piece of metal on the anvil's horn and hammer it with consistent strikes to bend it. Use the horn to create a hook shape.

After reheating, grip your piece firmly on the vise —make sure the punched hole is on top. With the twisting wrench jaws, hold your piece just under the shoulder and twist it.

Hold your metal piece with a vise and twist it

Step 7

When a piece of metal is heated repeatedly, it develops a slag layer. Use a wire brush to scrape it off.

To protect your hook from rust and corrosion, immerse it in oil until it is completely covered and then hold it near the forge until it changes to a dull black color.

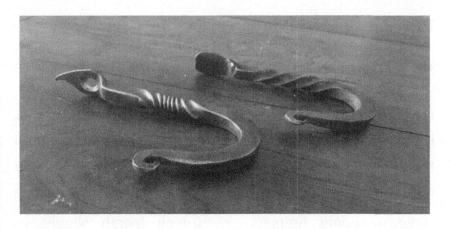

Treat your hook with oil to prevent rust, corrosion and then heat it to a dull black color

Step 8

Your J-hook is now ready for installation. Using the hole you created, screw it on the wall upright.

Project 2: Fire Poker

Step One

Look for a round piece of metal rod, preferably steel, because it can handle the heat from a fire. Cut your rod using a hacksaw to the required length. For example, if your poker is for a fire pit, you can use a 32-inch rod. If it is for a wood stove or home fireplace, a 20-inch length should be sufficient.

Take a file and round off both ends of your rod after trimming. You can also clean it to remove rust or chipping paint —if using a recycled piece such as an old tire iron rod.

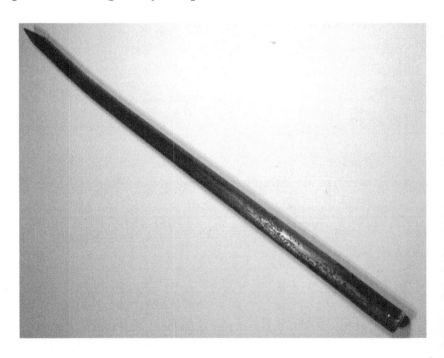

A metal rod like the one above is ideal for making a fire poker

Step 2

The second step involves attaching a heat-proof handle. Here, you can attach a wooden, hollow handle using glue or use a product called Sugru, a moldable glue that contains silicone and other additives. It comes in a packet and is similar to putty or clay. All you need to do is open the pack, roll your rod around it, and watch as it forms a heat-resistant handle. You can also buy different colors and mix them to customize your handle.

The moldable Sugru that contains silicone and other components

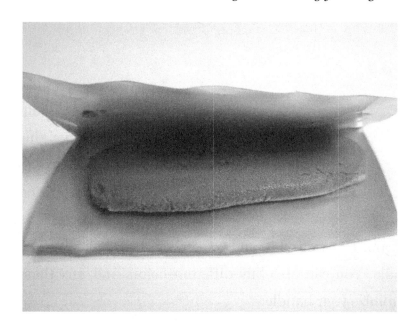

Sugru as it appears after opening the pack

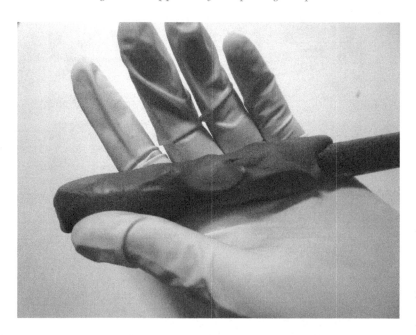

Place the Sugru around the handle

Roll the metal on a surface to create the handle and make it stick to your rod

Step 3

You can forge the rod and bend it to create a hook

To enable your fire poker to stir up or move logs, charcoal, and poke the fire, your rod needs a hook on the other end. There are two ways to achieve this. First, you can forge the end of the rod, then slightly bend by hammering it. Secondly, you can attach another small piece of metal close to the end of the rod that can stir up the fire.

Attach a hook close to the end of the poker to enable you easily hook and move various fuels

It is also possible to forge the end of the poker and create a hook to poke the fire

If you choose to attach a hook, use the forge welding process we learned earlier.

Step 4

To protect against extreme temperatures, you can protect your fire poker using the hard treatment to ensure durability and give it a rustic appearance. However, this is optional.

Step 5

Your poker is now complete and ready to stir fires and keep them burning.

Project 3: Twist-Forged Bracelet

Step 1

Heat one end of your piece of metal in the forge to a bright orange color. Once it is ready, place it on the anvil. Begin tapering the hot end by hammering it and turning it at 90° degree angles after each strike. Then, lay it flat on the anvil and strike again on the edge until it is 1 ½ inch long.

Forge the edges of your piece in preparation to shape the metal

Return your piece to the forge and repeat the above process on the other end of your piece. Once completed, straighten any bends, quench, and then dry it.

Step 2

Using a ruler, measure the entire length of your tapered piece of metal, and mark the center. Create a punch mark at the center and proceed to mark an inch on each side of your piece, starting from the middle part you marked initially.

Place your piece of metal back in the forge and let it heat to a bright orange color. While it heats, prepare a twisting tool and keep the vise within reach. Once your metal is ready, retrieve it and quickly secure it with the vise on one end, up to the punch marks at the center you marked. You have to work fast before it cools.

Take the twisting wrench and place it at the point of the second punch mark. Ensure both handles are straight and parallel to the floor. Twist one full turn, return your piece to the forge and heat it to bright orange again.

Twist your piece with a wrench while secured by a vise

Step 3

When your piece is hot enough, place it on the face of the anvil and leave about half an inch protruding from the anvil's edge. Hammer it until it forms an L-shape. Create a little scroll by rotating it 180°; the L should face up. Reheat once more, this time, the opposite end of your piece. Next, place it again on the anvil, with half an inch jutting out, and repeat the process – reheat when done.

Step 4

Hold your piece with tongs and place it on the tip of the anvil's horn. Ensure that only the scroll is hanging out.

Hammer the protruding part using measured blows while moving the piece a quarter of an inch with each strike. Stop hammering once you reach the twist and scroll, which are around one inch from the middle. Return your piece to the forge and repeat the process starting from the opposite tip.

Step 5

Take a wire brush and remove any accumulated slag. Dip your entire finished bracelet in oil for protection, and hold it with tongs next to the forge until it is dull black.

You can now wear your bracelet or gift it out.

The completed bracelet

Project 4: Fork

Step 1

A 4-6-inch bar of ¼ X ½ inches is ideal for this project. Using a center punch, create two marks on the edge of your piece; one on the tail end and the other two inches from the outer margin. Using tongs, place the marked end in the forge.

After heating, place your piece on the anvil at a tapering angle and hammer until it is 3/16 of an inch. From the center punch, taper one inch and maintain the thickness to ¼ of an inch.

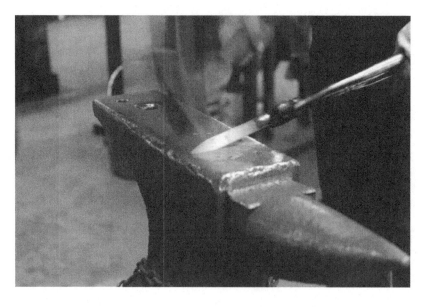

Forge your piece and taper the handle

Step 2

Place the edge of your piece on the anvil's horn and create the fork's neck to half an inch on one side, then hammer to flatten the neck to a quarter of an inch. On the wide side of the neck, strike it to measure slightly less than half an inch. Next, use a flat face hammer to flatten all the faces of your piece.

Shape the neck of the fork using the anvil's horn

Step 3

Place your piece on the edge of the anvil's horn with the faceplate near the edge. Use the center punch marks to align the flat edge and mark it with the hot cut. Ensure the placement is in line, and then cut through the piece. Turn the

139

piece around and cut out until the point where the two incisions meet.

Step 4

Remove all the hot metal you have just cut from the anvil and turn your attention to the prongs you have created. Hammer one of the prongs until it bends to 90°. Turn it 180°and bend it half an inch away from the face. Taper and square the edges and adjust them from an eighth to 3/16 of an inch.

Create the prongs by cutting off all the metal in the middle of the front part of your piece

Place a mark on the length of your piece near the hardy hole. Work on the edges to an octagon shape and then round them.

Step 5

Create a Y-shape on the prongs by opening them up around 30°, which should be the same angle from the centerline. Move your piece to the horn of the anvil, place the Y-shaped part upside down, and hammer the end of the handle to shape the fork's union, then reheat.

Step 6

Scrape of the accumulated slag and give your fork your preferred finishing treatment. It is now ready to use.

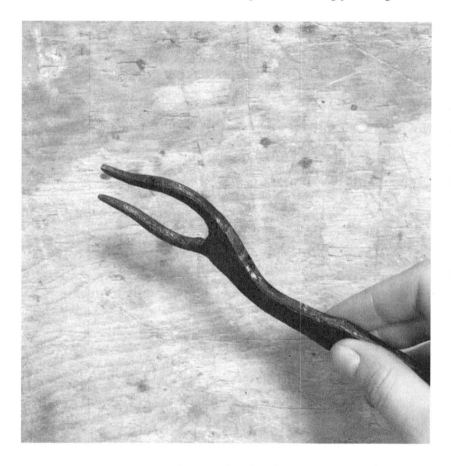

The completed fork

Project 5: Iron Necklace

Step 1

Instead of a piece of metal like other projects, you will require a long iron wire as the main raw material for this one. The tools required include a flat pair of pliers, a mandrel, a round nose, and snipers. A mandrel is a cylindrical rod that you will use to coil your wire.

Step 2

Coil your wire around the mandrel. The coiling does not have to be precise or in any particular order. The mandrel you use can also be made using any material, from wood to iron. The only important feature is that it must be cylindrical and placed in an upright position.

Coil your wire around the mandrel

Step 3

Once the entire iron wire is coiled, take your pliers and cut the now circular wire in a series of approximately after every two coils that go around the mandrel.

Alternatively, you can cut after every one complete coil and three quarters. The cut pieces will be in the form of circular coils. On each piece, create small circles on both ends of your wire using your round nose pliers.

Cut your wires in series

Step 4

On every circular piece, use your pliers to bend the coils at each of their halfway points, then insert them into each other, as illustrated in the photo.

Bend the coils in the middle

Close the circles you created at the ends of the pieces using your pliers. This acts as a lock to securely hold each of the interlocking coil bends.

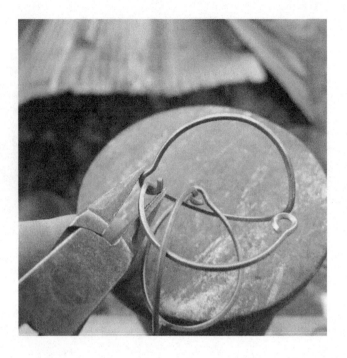

Use your pliers to close the edges of the coils

Step 5

Join as many circular coil pieces as you like depending on how long you want your necklace to be. Ensure you include a small ring and hook between each joining coil to hold them in place.

147

Join the coils together, depending on the intended length of your necklace

Use small rings to join the coils

Step 6

If the tail end of the chain circle is wide enough, instead of interlocking the coils, you can use other small rings to connect the circular pieces.

Add a hook and ring to enable closure

You can use any finishing treatment methods we learned earlier to complete your iron necklace.

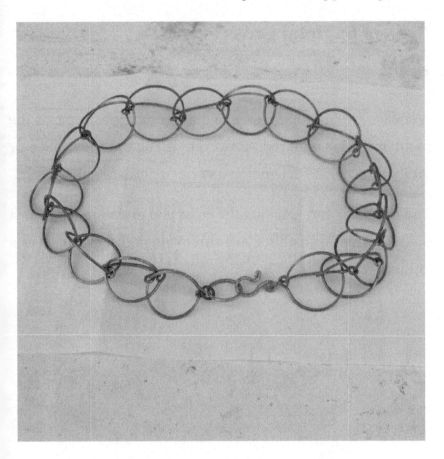

The complete iron necklace

Project 6: Metal Cross

Step 1

A square steel bar of between a quarter and 3/8 inches is the main material required. However, it can be in smaller or larger dimensions depending on size preference.

You can begin by sketching the cross you intend to make on a piece of paper with all the measurements indicated to act as a guide.

A square steel bar like the one shown above is an ideal piece beginning piece

Step 2

Forge your steel bar in readiness to work on it

Place your steel piece in the forge, heat to a yellow color, and when ready, place it on the anvil and bend it slightly at the center with a few hammer strikes. After achieving this, reheat and mount a cold chisel in the vise by the handle with the blade facing up.

Hold your piece of metal on the chisel's tip with tongs, and hammer it with measured strikes to split the steel bar to create arms for the cross. The split should spread upwards to about three-quarters of the bar's length.

Split your bar with a chisel to create the arms

Step 3

To increase the split, wiggle the tongs to increase leverage until the arms are spread out. In the process, the middle part may bend. Lay it on the anvil's face and tap the center part until it straightens out. The arms may also be leaning towards one side. Reheat if necessary and hammer them lightly to straighten them.

Wiggle your tongs to increase leverage and spread out the arms

Step 4

To remove vise markings, use a ball-peen hammer, after reheating, to create dimples across the face of your cross.

Depending on the size of the cross, smoothen and round any rough edges using a grinder or sandpaper.

Use a ball-peen hammer to remove any markings on the cross

Step 5

On the top part of the cross, drill a small hole that can host a wire loop or a wall hook if the cross will be hung on the wall. A wire loop comes in handy for a small-sized cross that can work as a key holder or neck chain.

Drill a hole on top of the cross to enable a hook or mounting

Step 6

Clean the cross with a wire brush and protect it from corrosion and other elements with an appropriate finishing treatment.

Project 7: Knife

Step 1

Grab your steel piece using tongs, place it in the forge, and heat it to a yellow color. After heating, place the piece flat on the anvil and begin to hammer it into the shape of a knife blade. You can achieve this by tapering the piece of steel on both sides.

Heat your piece to yellow to begin the knife-making process

Step 2

Flatten your piece by hammering the flat edge. This will create the cutting part of the knife, which you should do or the edges of both sides. Strike the edges until the two opposite sides are even. Technically, this process is called beveling, and the cut edges are called bevels.

Strike your hot piece to shape the blade

Step 3

To permanently maintain the newly created shape of the knife, heat your steel to a red color and wait for it to cool, then return it to the forge and heat again to a red color. Repeat this process three times. The heating and cooling ensure the knife's shape remains a permanent feature.

Step 4

Use sandpaper to smooth the piece of steel. After doing this, reheat and quench the knife in oil until it cools down to room temperature. Make sure you transfer the hot blade to the oil as fast as possible so that it hardens.

Smoothen your blade using sandpaper

Reheat your piece once again, but this time to a lower temperature to eradicate the stress and brittleness caused by the hardening process.

Step 5

Create a handle for the blade. There are several ways to do this; you can use Sugru, as we did with the fire poker, or you can pin and glue a wooden handle.

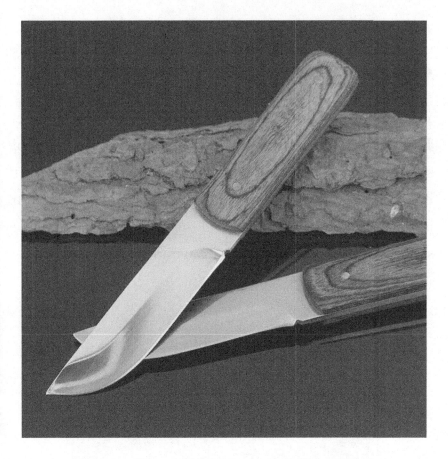

You can fix a ready-made wooden handle or Sugru

Step 6

Sharpen the knife's blade with a grinder or whetstone and clean it with running water to enhance its sharpness. Your knife is all set and ready for use.

Project 8: Hammer

Step 1

You need a block of steel at least 3X2 inches of any shape. This will serve as the hammer's head. Heat your lump of steel to orange, retrieve it and place it on the anvil. Hammer it to the shape you want your head to be. The most common is a square or round shape. Bevel the edges and work on the shape to ensure all the corners are symmetrical.

Use a block of steel to create the hammer's head.

Step 2

The next step involves punching the hole for the handle through the block. As you punch the hole or eye, rotate your piece of steel after every few strikes. This strategy ensures uniformity and compensates for any shortcomings in technique, material, or tools.

Drill a hole, known as the eye, through your piece to create room for the handle

Step 3

After the eye is complete, shape the cheeks of the head. Create two shallow throats a few inches from the head's edge on either side that go all the way around to transform your

163

piece of steel into a double-sided hammerhead. Although some blacksmiths use tongs for this task, a drift punch provides more accurate results.

Create the cheeks on both edges of your piece using a drift

Step 4

Ensure the middle part of your hammer and the eye is well-bolstered and hammered to the shape you want your final product to resemble. This includes the texture and thickness.

Step 5

Your hammerhead needs hardening owing to its job nature. It should handle endless blows delivered to tough and hot metal. The processes the head has undergone until this point may have caused stress. Heat the head to a high temperature, but instead of quenching, allow it to cool down slowly at room temperature to eradicate any stress.

Step 6

As it cools, it also provides an opportunity to stamp your signature or any other identifying mark on the head for posterity. Once it cools, you can slip on the handle of your choice and affix it tightly.

Brand your hammer

Project 9: Metal Spoon

Step 1

The piece of metal you can begin with and the spoon you can make out of that metal

Hold your metal piece against the far end of the anvil and taper it by hammering. Heat only half of your metal in the forge. Once it is ready, hold the metal with tongs and quench it up to the point where the jaws of the tongs begin to grip the piece.

Reheat and place the hot end of your piece on the anvil. Hammer the cold end until the hot end cools to a red color or bends. Roll it over, straighten, flatten and reheat it once more in the forge. Retrieve it when it is hot and continue upsetting using hard hammer strikes.

Step 2

Next, shape the ends of your metal piece into an octagon, and do not forget each edge should have two angles. Hammer to flatten and roll your metal piece over on the opposite side. Using the anvil's horn and a round-face hammer, strike the neck to reduce its thickness to 3/8 of an inch at its thinnest point.

Step 3

Return your piece to the forge and when you retrieve it, flatten the middle part by hammering. Work both sides to ¼ of an inch thickness. Use overlapping strikes to shape the handle and spread the edges. Using a flat-faced hammer, straighten all the faces or any high spots on your metal piece; flatten and spread the edges of your handle using overlapping strikes to 3/8 of an inch.

Step 4

With constant overlapping hammer hits, spread and flatten the edge to a thickness of 1/8 of an inch. Work on the neck using the anvil's horn and then place the flattened part over the hardy hole. Use a ball-peen hammer to sink it to a depth of between 1/3 - 3/8 of an inch. To achieve this, hammer between the two points in direct contact with the anvil's surface.

Work on shaping the handle and neck

Turn your attention to the flip side's edge and back. On the neck, bend your piece slightly and then place it over the edge of the anvil. Turn your piece 180° and set it on the anvil horn, upright on the tapered side. Hammer the piece until it is well-formed to your desired shape.

Step 5

Scrape off the slag with a wire brush and dip your spoon a few times in oil for increased protection. Hold it near the forge fire using tongs until it turns a dull black. Your spoon is now ready to use.

The final product

Project 10: Metal Bottle Opener

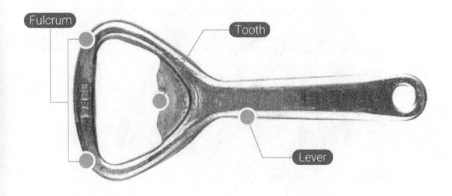

The main parts of a bottle opener

Step 1

Find a piece of metal exactly the size of your preferred bottle opener size. A popular standard size is 4-inches long and ¾ of an inch wide. Place your piece in the forge and heat it to a yellow color.

Begin with a piece of steel of the size you would like your opener to be

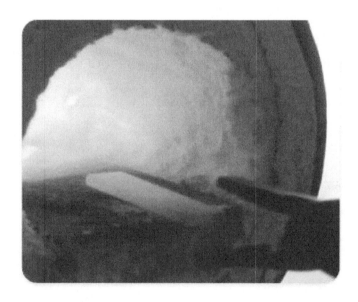

Heat your piece to yellow so you can work on it

Step 2

On one end of your piece, use a die cutter to create a small opening by cutting into the top part of the metal. This will serve as both the tooth and fulcrum of the bottle opener. Alternatively, you can look for a slot punch if a die cutter is not readily available.

Cut a space on the top part of your steel to serve as the fulcrum

Step 3

Shape the opening you created using a sheet of iron with several size holes or a dial-a-hole. Enlarge the opening by placing a drift into the fixed hole with your piece, place it above the size of the hole you want, and exert pressure or use light hammer taps. Stop when the enlarged opening can fit a bottle's mouth.

Create a sizeable hole on your piece

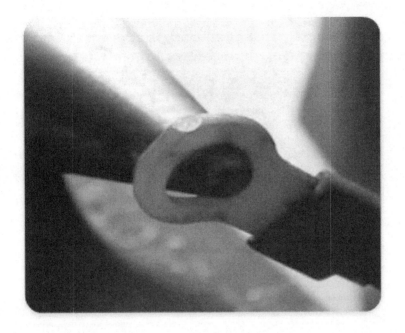

Widen the fulcrum to ensure it fits a bottle

Step 4

Hammer the inside and exterior corners to give the fulcrum a nice round shape. Once satisfied, curve out a tooth at the bottom of the circular opening hole using a drift.

Curve a tooth on the fulcrum

Reheat your piece and use a hammer to give the fulcrum and handle the final shape that you would like the opener to have.

Shape your opener to the shape you want while it is still hot.

Step 5

Allow the opener to cool, scrape off any slag, and then polish it with a rag for a clean and shiny finish. You can also give your bottle opener any finishing treatment you prefer.

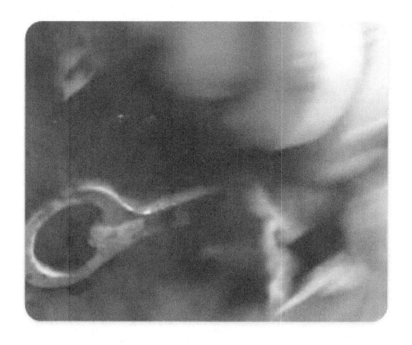

Clean your opener once it has cooled

Chapter 9: More Blacksmithing Projects

Project 11: Coil Spring Punch

Step 1

A punch is an essential tool for a blacksmith; its primary use is boring holes in metal. Instead of purchasing one, it is cheaper to make your own.

You need a rod of any size depending on the requirements of your projects; present and future. It is possible to make a punch out of an old coil spring or any other recycled piece of metal.

Begin by cutting your piece of rod to the size of the punch you require.

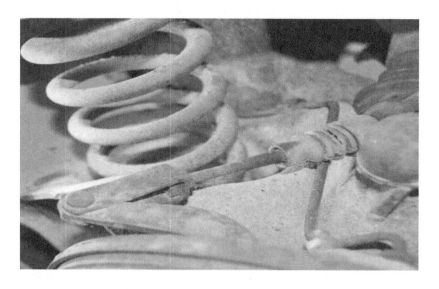

You can cut an old coil spring to get a rod for making a punch

Step 2

Heat your cut piece of metal to its respective forging temperature. Once ready, retrieve it from the forge, and place it on the anvil's face. Use a hammer to strike one end to taper it into a flat point. Turn your rod after every few blows to ensure the tapering is uniform, round off the edges, and create a rounded, sharp point.

Taper your rod to create a flat edge and then round them off to sharp points

Step 3

Complete the process by using a grinder to smoothen the punch. Alternatively, you can polish it for a shiny finish or leave it looking rough for a rustic appearance.

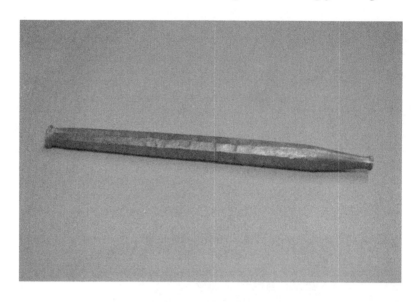

You can polish your completed punch or allow it to have an antique and rustic look

Project 12: Forged Leaf

Step 1

You can use quarter, half, or 3/8 inch round metal steel bars for this project.

Heat your bar, place it on an anvil, and hammer it to create a four-sided point on one of its edges. To achieve this, ensure you hold your piece at an angle so that your hammer can access both sides.

Hammer a four-sided point on your piece

Step 2

Reheat your piece and place it on the anvil with half of the four-sided points protruding while the other half rests on the anvil. Hammer the mid-point where your bar touches the anvil to create a shoulder. Turn your piece and do the same on the opposite side at 90° angles.

Hammer the point between the protruding edge and the part that rests on the anvil

Striking the mid-way point creates a shoulder

Round off the corners since the above process results in squared edges.

Step 3

Hammer the bulb formed on the edge of your piece by placing it on the side of the anvil's face. Angle the position slightly so that your piece creates a kind of ridge at its center. The strikes flatten the bulb and create a leaf shape.

Hammer the bulb to flatten it and create a leaf

Draw some veins using a rounded hot chisel, as illustrated below.

Creating imprints of the leaf's veins

After the vein imprints are complete

Step 4

Detach the leaf from the rest of your piece using a hot cut in place of a hammer. Cut the edge and leave a small piece attached, then use tongs to break the remaining bit of the leaf-free. This method keeps your edge from flying off due to the force exerted by a hammer.

Remove the leaf from the rod by heating it and cutting it off

Heat the stem attached to the leaf while holding the detached piece with tongs. First, hammer the edges to a blunt point, then an octagon, and lastly to a round shape.

Round off the edge of the stem

Step 5

Hammer the stem's rounded point into a small pigtail to prevent the edge from poking anybody. Create a back curve on the stem that extends to the center of the leaf's back.

Create a pigtail with the stem that bends back to the leaf

With a wire brush, clean the leaf of any forging residue while still hot.

Step 6

Polish the leaf to create a shiny appearance and allow it to dry. Your forged leaf is now complete.

Polish the leaf to a shiny silver finish

Project 13: Forged Metal Heart

Step 1

Use a piece of steel and begin by cutting it to a length of 15 inches. Measure the center, which should be at the 7.5-inch point, and mark it. You only require a tiny mark, and you can touch it lightly with an angle grinder.

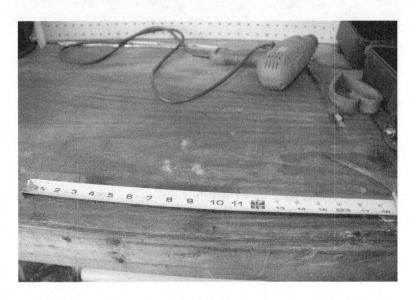

Measure a length of 15 inches and mark the halfway point of your piece

Step 2

Heat your piece of steel and bend it at the marked halfway point. Place the hot piece at the edge of the anvil at the center and lightly strike it with a hammer to curve it.

Bend your hot piece at the center

Step 3

Square the bend to a right angle by placing your piece at the far end of the anvil and hammering the edges of the corners.

Square the bend to a right angle

Step 4

Place one elbow of your piece on the anvil and strike it with a hammer to curve it. As you hammer, move the elbow slowly forward. Repeat the same process on the other elbow. This process will produce a heart shape.

If a gap remains at the top where the two elbows join, use tongs to squeeze both elbows and close the gap. This is the difficult part, and it requires patience to get the curves right.

Curve both elbows to create a heart shape

Step 5

When the steel is cool at room temperature, brush off the scale of the fire that makes the heart appear black. Use a finishing treatment of your choice to complete the project.

Brush and give the completed heart your preferred finishing treatment

Project 14: Simple Shield

Step 1

The main raw material you will require is a flat, clean sheet of steel. You can use other metal sheets, but steel is the best.

A steel sheet is the best material for building a shield

Make a life-size sketch of your shield's design on a piece of paper first with the actual measurements. This makes the process much simpler. It could be an original or existing design.

Design a sketch to simplify the process

Step 2

Get your hands on a marking tool that you can use to transfer your sketch onto the steel sheet. Transfer your sketch onto your sheet and cut it out as accurately as possible. Remember, precision in cutting is important as it influences the final result. Therefore, take your time and get the measurements right.

Use a grinder to smoothen the rough edges of your shield for an aesthetic look and prevent injuries from the sharp sides.

Grind the edges of your shield after cutting to make them smooth

Step 3

Join the various shield cuttings together to enable forging. You can use various methods such as taping to hold the pieces temporarily. After forging, you can use riveting or forge welding depending on the metal used and design. Place your shield on a roller to form a curved shape.

Step 4

Attach a handle on the inner side of your shield. You can make one from metal rods or steel —It has to be constructed from a durable material because the handle bears all of the shield's weight.

Step 5

Add a finishing treatment to give your shield a unique touch and make it stand out. It will also protect your shield from external elements and guarantee durability.

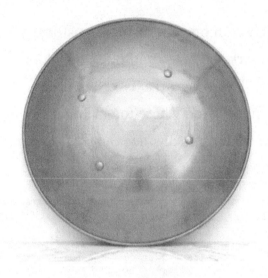

Give your shield finishing treatment once complete

Project 15: Tongs

Step 1

Use two lightweight metal pieces, approximately ¼ by ¾ by 8 inches in size.

Mark your piece on one end using soapstone; 1 ¼ inch from the edge to mark the jaws, and one inch from the jaw mark for the boss. The boss area is the part that immediately comes after the jaw and where tongs join. Also, mark the two points with a center punch since the soapstone markings will disappear once your piece is heated.

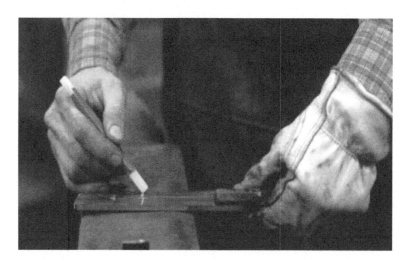

Mark your piece using soapstone to mark the boss and jaw.

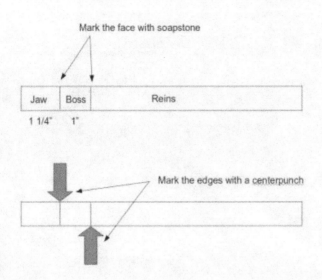

Mark the edges using a center punch as shown above since the soapstone markings will disappear once your piece is heated.

Step 2

Create two dents on opposite sides where the boss will be. The dents will later be transformed into round holes to host rivets. Work on the reins by drawing them out and hammering both sides of your piece to ensure they are the right length.

Create two dents on your piece where the boss should be

As you draw out the reins, round the corners and remove any hammer dents on your piece by heating it to a low temperature and then hammering the metal. This technique is called plenishing.

Step 3

Hold your two pieces side by side to compare their length. If one is longer than the other, draw out its length until both are identical.

Clamp your piece in the vise and at the junction between the jaw and the boss, make a short twist of 90°to shape the jaw, and repeat the same process with the second piece. Always ensure both pieces are twisted in the same direction.

Clamp each piece and twist to 90° to shape the jaw

Step 4

Place each of the hot pieces on the anvil and smoothen the corners of the twist to ensure the boss and jaw are square and smooth.

With a center punch, mark the rivet holes and cut the holes with a slitter. Ensure the slitter is approximately 3% larger than the rivet to make up for shrinkage when the rivet cools. Turn your piece on the opposite side and cut the hole by driving the slitter through.

Drive a drift through and smoothen the rivet hole you have just made; alternate between both sides of the hole.

Drive the slitter through the hole

Step 5

Heat the rivet in the forge. It should be one and a half times the diameter of the rivet hole and have the length to go through both your metal pieces.

Insert the red hot rivet through the hole in the pieces and hammer it down.

Insert the heated rivet through the hole

Step 6

Once the rivet is fixed, the tong joints will be too tight to move. To correct this and free up the joint, heat them and open and close the tongs several times until the joint loosens up.

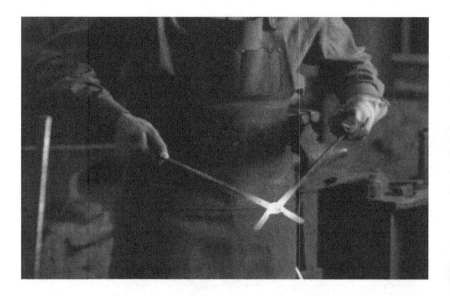

Play with the joint until it loosens up

Place your tongs in the vise and align the reins while fitting them to the stock's size.

Next, quench your tongs while opening and closing the joint repeatedly.

Quench your tongs as you open and close the joint repeatedly

Once they cool, your pair of tongs will be ready for use.

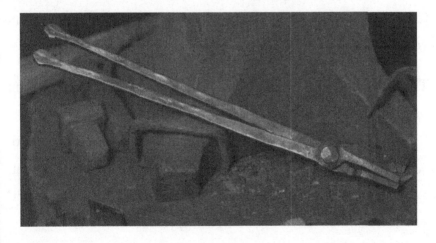

The finished pair of tongs

Final Word

In the past, blacksmiths were the cornerstone of every community. They ensured a community could protect itself by ensuring weapons were readily available, created farm tools for communities to be food secure, and made sure the wagons for transport had wheels and other components – easing mobility. Though times have changed, nothing has diminished the important role of blacksmiths in the 21st Century.

The satisfaction of designing and creating your own products instead of buying them is priceless, and the fascination of taking a plain piece of iron and transforming it into an item you have always required is unmatched.

The rewards extend to your financials because once you begin forging metal and creating products, family and close friends will probably start placing orders for items they need. Advertising your products is also easier with the internet. With time, you may have a fully-fledged, full-time, and profitable business doing something you love.

Since blacksmithing is a physically demanding craft, it ensures you always maintain fitness and build strength – which is healthy. This ancient craft also instills discipline and patience, which are important virtues. Discipline comes because you have to tirelessly shape an item until it takes the form you had intended. Patience arises from learning how to give the numerous techniques and processes time, attention to detail, and focus, thereby ensuring you can achieve the desired results.

This is what makes blacksmithing a little more special compared to other hobbies or careers – the benefits traverse the body, mind, and soul. It also means you can never go wrong by learning blacksmithing skills.

PS: I'd like your feedback. If you are happy with this book, please leave a review on Amazon.

Please leave a review for this book on Amazon by visiting the page below:

https://amzn.to/2VMR5qr

Made in the USA
Las Vegas, NV
13 December 2023

82672267R00118